AF223382

Hans-Hermann Seiffert
The Lost Race against Time during "The Final Solution"

Hans-Hermann Seiffert

Translated into English by Uta Allers

The Lost Race against Time during "The Final Solution"

The Emigration of the Jewish Families Guggenheim of Konstanz and Rosenwald of Cologne to Argentina and the USA Fails in 1938 - 1942

Hartung-Gorre Publisher, Konstanz

Front cover: (upper row, left: Toni Guggenheim, Lisel Rosenwald, Johanna Rosenwald; bottom row, left: Salomon Guggenheim, Karl Rosenwald, Dagobert Guggenheim) (Photo source: Guggenheim and Fradkin photos). Back cover: *Stolpersteine* in the Konstanz Hüetlinstraße 21, upper row, (Photo credit: H.-H. Seiffert) and in the Cologne Antwerpenerstraße 32 bottom row (Photo: https://de.wikipedia.org/wiki/Liste_der_Stolpersteine_im_Kölner_Stadtteil_Neustadt-Nord).

1939-2019
80 Years Beginning of World War II and of the Extermination of European Jews by the German Nazi Government

Bibliographic information published by Die Deutsche National-bibliothek

Die Deutsche Nationalbibliothek lists this publication in the Deutsche Nationalbibliografie; detailed bibliographic data is available in the internet at http://dnb.ddb.de.

1st Edition 2019 / Erste Auflage 2019
Hartung-Gorre Verlag, Konstanz, Germany
ISBN 3-86628-661-9 / 978-3-86628-661-0

Contents

An Unexpected Discovery of Clues

The book about the fate of the Guggenheim family of Konstanz, launched in the spring of 2010 with the title "In Argentinien gerettet – in Auschwitz ermordet" ("Saved in Argentina – Murdered in Auschwitz"), seemed to have been completed. All the documents, which had been found during a two-year intensive search of various archives and memorial sites, had been checked and the results shared in interviews with the descendants in Argentina.

Admittedly, there were scant document to be had, since the letters between the interned Guggenheim family members and their relatives – now safe in Argentina – were no longer available; they had simply been lost. The lack of any correspondence from Camp Gurs, Camp Les Milles and Marseille to Buenos Aires is particularly unfortunate. Of course, the letters going the other way disappeared with the murder of Salomon, Toni and Dagobert Guggenheim in Auschwitz. The life of the three Guggenheims and the way to their destruction could be considered fully researched, given the lack of further evidence at the time.

So it was a big surprise when, in June 2017, more than seven years after the publication of the book, a Jewish woman with German ancestors contacted the author from abroad; she expressed a keen interest in the documentation of the fate of the Guggenheim families of Konstanz and Donaueschingen. This contact was doubly surprising: for one thing, this person – Joan Rosenwald-Fradkin – got in touch not from Argentina, but from the USA, and her ancestors came not from Konstanz or Donaueschingen, but from Cologne.

The other astonishing fact was that Joan's father and aunt, the siblings Fritz and Lisel Rosenwald, had a close relationship with both Guggenheim families. Fritz Rosenwald had become friends with Isi Guggenheim during his three-year position with a Konstanz company, while his sister Lisel had a romantic relationship with Dagobert Guggenheim. These connections were neither documented in the available papers, nor did the descendants in Buenos Aires know about them.

It turned out to be a special stroke of luck that the abundance of letters – a total of over 300 – written by Lisel and her parents in Cologne to their brother and son Fritz, who emigrated to New York City in 1938, had been preserved. It is especially the letters of Lisel, written to her brother every week from 1938 until her deportation at the end of 1941, that provide previously unknown details. Key among them are the emigration efforts of the Guggenheims waiting in Konstanz and Lisel's relationship with Dagobert.

The letters give an in-depth look into the emotional life of the Guggenheim and Rosenwald family members, as they desperately struggled to reach "safe harbors" abroad. Their hopes, their fears, their disappointments – all come to the fore in these letters. The reports also make clear the amount of time and the financial expenses Fritz Rosenwald devoted to overcoming the obstacles that kept getting in his sister's way on the American side of the Atlantic. All this, while he was just getting settled in the USA. Right at the end, just before their deportation to Riga, Fritz receives the heartfelt gratitude of his family.

It is especially touching that the siblings never reproach each other during all the dashed hopes, but instead, continue to give each other encouragement. Remarkable, too, is how the parents and sister, though being subjected to discrimination and harassment in Cologne, are concerned about Fritz establishing himself professionally in his new residence – New York City – and wanting him to have leisure time to enjoy his freedom. In short: the letters are an expression of a loving connection between the Rosenwald parents and children, especially between brother and sister.

The insights from the letters into the relationships between the Guggenheim and Rosenwald families, their shared struggles and defeats in trying to escape the Nazi's "Final Solution", as well as Lisel Rosenwald's courageous attitude throughout, have prompted the author to revise this book in an expanded form.

I extend a special thank you to Joan Fradkin and other members of the Rosenwald family for providing all the documents and photos so helpful for this presentation.

Konstanz, April 2019
Hans-Hermann Seiffert

Forword of the Rosenwald Family

During my childhood in the 1950s and 1960s, my parents, Fred and Ruth Rosenwald spoke very little about our relatives who perished during the Holocaust. While I wanted to know more about our missing relatives, I knew not to ask my parents about them.

As a child, I was particularly interested in knowing what happened to my father's side of the family. I hoped that maybe somehow my father's mother, Johanna Rosenwald and his sister, Liesel had survived the Holocaust. Even though I never met them, I wanted them to be a part of our lives.

In 2013, my brother and I donated the 1938 through 1941 letters primarily written by my father's mother and sister to the United States Holocaust Memorial Museum. The recipient of these letters was my father who was then living in NYC. He had emigrated from Germany to the USA in early 1938. My father kept these letters until his death when they were passed on to my mother. Upon the death of my mother, my brother and I inherited them.

In 2017, some of the letters were translated from German into English by the United States Holocaust Memorial Museum and a biographical list of some people mentioned in the letters was also prepared. It is through these materials that I began to find out about the Guggenheim and Rosenwald connection. Through the materials, I also came into contact with Hans-Hermann Seiffert and he sent me a copy of his original Guggenheim book, *In Argentinien gerettet – in Auschwitz ermordet*. Amazingly, the book contained pictures of some of the Guggenheims that matched some of the photos in my father's photo album.

Thanks to the diligence of Hans-Hermann Seiffert, we now have the updated version of the original book which includes the missing pieces of the story. My family and I are grateful to Hans for what he has done.

I hope that people learn from this book not to prejudge others based upon their faith, ethnicity, culture, etc. We are much more alike than different. I, myself, try to honor those who perished by being a kind, fair and honorable person. They live in my heart.

New York, October 2019
Joan Fradkin-Rosenwald

Appreciation

The process of transforming a family's fate into a book about events from many years ago calls for the collaboration of many heads and hands, especially with document research.

In this regard, my special thanks go to Gabriela Guggenheim and Beatriz Strauss, the second- and third-generation survivors of the two Guggenheim families of Konstanz and Donaueschingen, living in Argentina. Both were happy to make available to the author all remaining documents that provided information about their ancestors' lives before and during the persecution of the Nazi regime.

I would also like to thank Professor Erika Rosenberg in Buenos Aires, who was helpful in the search for the descendants there.

With great interest and dedication, Mr. Raimund Adamczyk, Director of the City Archives of Donaueschingen, and Ms. Sandra Nagel of the Musée Mémorial de la Shoah in Paris worked with me in assisting with the research. For that, I give my heartfelt thanks!

I received valuable support from other sources with editorial terms, proofreading and, not least, computer processing. I am grateful to all those who contributed.

Konstanz, February 2010
Hans-Hermann Seiffert

"Les déportés ont connu la plus fantastique
entreprise de déshumanisation et
d'extermination de l'Histoire."

[The deportees experienced the most incredible
project of dehumanization and
extermination in history.]

André Chipot, André Rogerie
(Déportés Résistants)[1]

---

[1] Preface by Suzanne Birnbaum, *Une Francaise juive est revenue* (Paris: Hérault Éditions, 1989)

A Difficult Search for Clues After 70 Years

All the members of the related Guggenheim families of Konstanz and Donaueschingen who still remained in Germany at the end of the 1930s left the country from Konstanz. Some fled on their own initiative in their flight from the Nazis; they emigrated to Argentina. The others were deported, expatriated to southwest France and later murdered in Auschwitz.

Consequently, the murdered family members belong to the six million European Jews who became the victims of the Holocaust, which was one of the Nazi regime's formulated and rigorously enforced state goals. The number *six million* stands for anonymity and may lead to the assumption that all the victims suffered the same fate in a killing procedure that was largely carried out bureaucratically and technologically. Such a general point of view of excluding the individuality of each person's fate makes it harder, however, to grasp the dimensions of this crime by the state and to evoke the appropriate compassion.

Researching their individual fates makes clear that each victim experienced the time of persecution differently and suffered accordingly. We are dealing with six million people who became victims of this genocide. Each victim had his or her own individual biography, history, expectations of life, hopes and disappointments.

The laying of individual memorial stones for the victims of the Nazi regime through the *Konstanzer Initiative Stolpersteine* offered the impetus for a last comprehensive research detailing the persecution of the two Jewish families of Salomon and Abraham Guggenheim. This author took on this project with high hopes but soon faced imminent failure. He found very few clues in the local archives about the Salomon Guggenheim family, who were apparently living very inconspicuously in Konstanz, as well as their Donaueschingen relatives. Due to a lack of photo materials, all these people remained faceless for the time being. Only through detours and coincidence was it possible to establish contact with the surviving relatives of the Konstanz and Donaueschingen Guggenheims, now living in Argentina. Only with the family photos provided by their children, grandchildren and great-grandchildren could the "anonymous" family members – some murdered and others forced to emigrate – be identified.

The author did, however, have the same experience as many historians who question the descendants of the Jewish victims about the fates of their families. These descendants can often report very little or nothing, because nothing was shared about the persecution, victimization and experiences in the camps. Withholding such information was thought to help the survivor cope with that personal history, but also, and not least, to prevent burdening the lives of the descendants with their parents' memories and suffering.

It is especially unfortunate that not a single letter or postcard was saved, which family members Salomon, Toni and Dagobert Guggenheim must have written while interned in France to the relatives who emigrated to Argentina. Such correspondence would have provided information about the state of mind, the hopes and fears that those interned in the Gurs and Les Milles camps experienced.

Consequently, the author then had to rely solely on the results of an arduous search for clues in the French internment camps archives, the Yad Vashem Holocaust Remembrance Center (Jerusalem) and the German archives. From the mosaic pieces gathered in this way, he was able to put together a documentation. Although certain life stages still remained in fragmentary form, his research nevertheless fairly accurately portrayed the sequence of events for the most significant parts of the ordeal that led to the murder of the couple, Toni and Salomon Guggenheim, and their nephew, Dagobert.

"In Argentinien gerettet – in Auschwitz ermordet"

Konstanz, February 2010
Hans-Hermann Seiffert

Entrance gate and ramp at Auschwitz-Birkenau, 2008 (Photo courtesy of Erhard Roy Wiehn)

Forcibly Driven to Emigration and Death

In the city of Konstanz, Jews had been registered since 1242, were expelled in 1537, and only after 1847 were they allowed to settle there again. The new Konstanz Jewish Community was founded in 1866; the synagogue was dedicated in 1883, damaged in 1936, and totally destroyed on November 9/10, 1938, later known as Pogromnacht or Kritallnacht. Jews were deported to the Dachau concentration camp, and the community was gutted by the deportation of the last Jewish residents to Camp de Gurs in southwest France on October 22, 1940. In Gailingen on the Hochrhein (see chapter "From the Jewish Villages …"), there is evidence of Jewish families as early as 1654-1657. By 1700 there was a prayer room or chapel; by 1766 a synagogue; by 1815 a Jewish elementary school; by 1827 the headquarters of a district rabbinate; by 1847 a *mikvah* (ritual bath); and by 1858 the Jewish population was just over 50 percent of the village's total. In 1866, the new synagogue was dedicated. From 1870 to 1884, Leopold Guggenheim was the mayor, and by 1898 there was a Jewish Home for the Aged. In November 1938 the synagogue was destroyed, and the Jews were persecuted in Dachau. On October 22, 1940, all remaining Jewish residents were deported to Gurs, an act that violently ended Jewish life there that spanned almost 300 years. Jewish families had been living in the Hegau village of Randegg (see "From the Jewish Villages …") since 1656; and there was a synagogue since about 1810. In 1825 there were precisely 289 (40.5%) Jewish residents, and by 1885 they numbered 252 (27.4%) of 921 residents. There were Jewish schools and a village rabbi. In November 1938 the old synagogue was destroyed, and Jews were tortured in Dachau. With the last Jewish residents deported to Gurs in October 22, 1940, the Jewish community in Randegg was completely destroyed. In Donaueschingen (see "From the Jewish Villages. …"), in 1933 there were only 18 Jews out of 5,440 residents, 14 of whom soon emigrated, with the remaining four people leaving the city after November 1938. Jews had the right to settle in the Grand Duchy of Baden since 1808 and since 1809 had the status of a religious community. By 1828 there was tax equalization, by 1849 access to civil service, and by 1862 Jews were granted full legal equality. By 1900 Baden had 26,135 Jewish citizens (1.7% of the population). In less than seven years as of 1933, many centuries of Jewish tradition were destroyed and with it, thousands upon thousands of totally innocent human beings – *only because they were Jewish.*

After his exemplary work about the fate of the Jewish Hammel family of Konstanz, Hans-Hermann Seiffert has now commendably researched and documented the divergent fates of the Salomon Guggenheim family of Konstanz and the Abraham Guggenheim family of Donaueschingen. Salomon Guggenheim (born 1877 in Randegg) and his wife Toni (born 1891 in Gailingen) were deported from Konstanz on October 22, 1940 to the Gurs internment camp in southwest France. On August 16, 1942, they were murdered in Auschwitz-Birkenau, along with their nephew Dagobert (born 1910 in Donaueschingen, son of Bona and Abraham Guggenheim). Erna Strauss, Bona's daughter, had already emigrated with her husband and son to Argentina in 1935. Isi Guggenheim (born 1915 in Konstanz, son of Salomon and Toni Guggenheim) arrived in the safe haven of Argentina in June 1938 and died in Buenos Aires in May 2000. Bona Guggenheim (née Jung in 1881 in Gailingen; Toni's sister) was able to save herself in Argentina with the help of her daughter Erna and died in Buenos Aires in 1952.

Along with many other aspects of these families'ordeals, Hans-Hermann Seiffert makes very clear how the employees of the Konstanz passport office and other local agencies abetted the murder of Dagobert, Toni and Salomon Guggenheim – and possibly not only those three – as "office perpetrators" working within the scope of the "Final Solution" that was carried out by the state bureaucracies. This complicity was never atoned for. Whether these accomplices were ever cognizant of their atrocious deeds after 1945 and perhaps at least regretted them will forever remain their secret. Especially disgraceful was the so-called "restitution" described by the author, as exemplified in the case of the surviving Guggenheims, subjected as they were to blatant non-restitution. The stunningly simple explanation for this is that the civil servants and other employees responsible for these matters after 1945 were, for the most part, the same employee abettors as in the 1930s, especially in the courts, but not only there.

Hans-Hermann Seiffert deserves our sincere gratitude for his carefully researched and fascinating memorial work, by which he restored the names and faces to those who were robbed of all their rights, had all their property confiscated and, finally, were forcibly driven to emigration and death, *because they were Jews*. Seventy years after the barbaric deportation by Germans of the Jewish Germans – the aged, young, sick, women, men – from southwest Germany to Gurs as a first destination on the way to Auschwitz-Birkenau, this documentation by Hans-Hermann Seiffert stands as a substantial contribution to counter the memory loss about the local and regional dimensions of the Shoah in Konstanz and Donaueschingen in Germany and the world. The world will hopefully not soon forget what is written, published and stored in various libraries.

March 17, 2010; Erhard Roy Wiehn

Hans-Hermann Seiffert

The Lost Race Against Time during "The Final Solution"

A Municipal Department as Accomplice to the State's Extermination Policy

In mid-1941, Salomon Guggenheim found himself in a castaway's mode: envisioning the coast of a safe haven yet repeatedly driven back to the open ocean by treacherous currents. The "safe haven" was a steamship passage that could take him and his wife Toni from their internment in France to Argentina. There, the Jewish couple would be safe from the persecution of the German dictators. In Argentina, their son Isi, having already left Konstanz in 1938, was trying hard to clear all the bureaucratic hurdles for his parents' legal entry to Buenos Aires. But from Argentina he was unable to remove the one obstacle that caused the undertaking to fail.

Toni and Salomon Guggenheim around the end of the 1930s (Photo courtesy of Gabriela Guggenheim)

Despite several requests, the Passport Office in their hometown of Konstanz was not willing to return the passports taken from the Jews upon deportation in October 1940, thereby denying them the necessary entry visa for emigration from France.[2] By so doing, the local administration in Konstanz contributed its macabre part in depriving the city's already deported and expatriated former residents of their last chance of survival,.

A year later in August 1942, Salomon and Toni Guggenheim were deported to Auschwitz-Birkenau in the course of the so-called "Final Solution of the Jewish Question" – also being carried out then in the unoccupied part of France – and were murdered in a gas chamber.

On the same train transport from Drancy near Paris to Auschwitz was their nephew, Dagobert, son of Bona and Abraham, the Donaueschingen relatives of the Konstanz Guggenheims. Dagobert had supported his aunt and uncle during the past few years and had accompanied them on all the way stations since their deportation to southern France. He, too, did not survive the deportation. It may be assumed that Dagobert was assigned to a forced labor crew in Auschwitz upon arrival. Not known, however, is when and how he died.

Dagobert Guggenheim, end of the 1920s (Photo courtesy of Beatriz Strauss)

---

[2] Letter by Salomon Guggenheim of July 1, 1941 to Erna Veit, Kreuzlingen (Switzerland). (Yad Vashem Archives, Jerusalem).

At the time of Dagobert's and her parents' death, Lisel Rosenwald, Dagobert's fiancée, was still in the Riga Ghetto. The Jewish woman from Cologne was deported with her parents, Carl and Johanna Rosenwald, on December 7, 1941 to the Riga ghetto in the course of the massive deportation campaign of the Jews still remaining in the Greater German Reich. Her immigration efforts of several years to the "safe harbor" of New York, too, had failed.

While it may be assumed that her parents soon died in Riga, Lisel was able to survive more than three years of being imprisoned by the German "Master Race". She died in the Stutthof camp on January 6, 1945 at the age of thirty.

With that, she, like her parents and the Guggenheims before her, lost the race against time during the "Final Solution".

From the Jewish Villages of Hegau to the City of Konstanz on Lake Constance

Who were these Guggenheims and what role did they play in the lives of their hometown communities of Konstanz and Donaueschingen?

Salomon and Toni Guggenheim were among those Jews who had moved with their Jewish community from the rural communities of Hegau and the peninsula Höri to the city of Konstanz, which had grown rapidly since the end of the 19th century. Salomon came from the Hegau village Randegg where he was born on September 27, 1877, the son of the tradesman Isak and his wife Sophie, née Rothschild. As the streets and paths in Randegg did not have names back then, the birth address was given only as House No. 14. Today the house is on the Otto-Dix Straße with the number 34. Salomon had three siblings, two older sisters Adele and Anna, as well as a younger brother Siegfried. It is known that Adele and Siegfried died during the course of the October 1940 deportation while confined in the Gurs internment camp.

Salomon moved to Konstanz in 1912. His first residence was in Hüetlinstraße 17, where he opened an ironware store. A year later, he married Toni Jung and moved with her in April 1913 to a four-room apartment in the third story of Hüetlinstraße 21. After the outbreak of World War I, he, like most of the Jewish men, served in the German military.

However, there is only scant information about his wartime service in the available documents.[3] His unit and its locations are also unknown.

His wife Toni, born June 29, 1891, and thereby 14 years younger than her husband, came from Gailingen, the next village over from Randegg. At that time, the Gailingen community had an unusually high Jewish population and represented a powerhouse in the Jewish life in Germany's rural southwest. For 14 years from 1870 to 1884, a Jewish mayor named Leopold Guggenheim even held office there.

Toni was the daughter of Daniel Jung, also a businessman, and his wife Klara, née Weil. Two other children – Jakob, who died in World War I, and the oldest daughter Bona, born in 1881 – made up the Jung family.

Toni and Salomon's only child, son Isi, was born in Konstanz at Hüetlinstraße 21 on April 20, 1915. After completing elementary school, Isi, given his parents' business activities, was predestined to begin a commercial career. He completed his secondary schooling at the Konstanz Zeppelin-Oberreal School, and then went on to three years of commercial training from 1931 to 1934 in the Hermann Einstein fabric and lingerie store in the Bodanstraße. While working, Isi successfully completed one-year professional training in the Höheren Handelschule (a commercial college). Upon completing the training, Isi was hired by the Einstein Company as assistant to the management with operational tasks in sales.

Isi Guggenheim, mid-1930s (Photo courtesy of Gabriela Guggenheim)

---

[3] Response of the administration at Camp Gurs to a February 1941 request to the Prefecture des Départements Basses Pyrénées about the transfer of Salomon and Toni Guggenheim to Les Milles (Archives Départementales (AD) Basses Pyrénées, Pau.)

Isi's career development led him to Donaueschingen. Being employed by the Einstein Company had advantages, given the long-time professional connection that the owner, Hermann Einstein, had built with Abraham Guggenheim, Isi's uncle in Donaueschingen.

Hermann Einstein's store, Bodanstraße 22 in Konstanz (Photo source: D. Schott/W. Trapp, *Konstanz in den 20er und 30er Jahren* [Konstanz in the 1920s and 1930s])

Donaueschingen as the Center of a Small Group of Department Stores

Dagobert, the third victim of the Guggenheim family clan, grew up on the edge of the Black Forest in Donaueschingen. Like Isi, his cousin five years younger, he also chose the career of retail salesman after completing secondary school. His future was more assured after his training, because he could count on taking over the ownership of one of the Guggenheim department stores in Donaueschingen, Singen and Gaggenau, in which his parents were partners.

The Guggenheim department store when founded in 1897 in Donaueschingen, Wasserstraße (Photo source: Willi Hönle)

Dagobert's parents – mother Bona, née Jung, and father Abraham Guggenheim – both came from Gailingen. Abraham built his professional livelihood at a young age. In 1897, at age 23, he founded the Kaufhaus Guggenheim & Cie. [Guggenheim and Co. department store] with the Konstanz businessman Hermann Einstein in the Donaueschingen Wasserstraße and lived as a tenant in House #290 next to the commercial space. After obtaining property along with his associate Hermann Einstein in the neighboring Eisenbahnstraße, the business and the living quarters were moved to the much larger space there. The impressive building was characterized on the outside by beautiful window arcades and on the inside by an open-space design.[4] In 1908, the street was renamed and from then on the business address was Max-Egon-Straße 14.

---

[4] The building was partially destroyed in bombing attacks in 1945. See Volkhard Huth, in *"Erinnerung und Gegenwart"*, *Historischer Wegweiser durch Donaueschingen* ["Memories and the Present," *Historic Guide Through Donaueschingen*], City of Donaueschingen, 1992, p. 45.

Kaufhaus [Department Store] Guggenheim, newly built in the Max-Egon-Straße
(Photo source: Donaueschingen City Archives)

In March 1899, additional branches were established in Singen Scheffelstraße 6 and in October 1900 in Gaggenau Hauptstraße 31a. In Singen, the company moved in November 1912 into a newly built commercial and residential building in Scheffelstraße 15 that was financed with a mortgage by two commercial backers living in London, the Max Frank and Emil Kaiser Jewish families, both related to Einstein.[5]

In Donaueschingen, the Guggenheim family was complete with the birth of daughter Erna in September 1905 and son Dagobert in July 1910.

---

[5] Reinhild Kappes, ... *Und in Singen gab es keine Juden? (And in Singen There Were No Jews?)* (Sigmaringen: Jan Thorbecke Publisher, 1991), pp. 27; 29.

Erna Strauss, née Guggenheim (Photo courtesy of Beatriz Strauss)

The business continued to grow: The simple notions store grew into a textile clothing department store with a broad assortment and a greatly expanded clientele. With the entry of Emil Frank of Konstanz as a personally liable shareholder, who provided additional collateral, the owners took on further business risks. With good service, high quality awareness and reasonable prices, the department store succeeded in becoming the market leader in the textile clothing trade. Under the assertive motto *"Guggenheim always in the lead!"* the business used a new, original publicity strategy:

"With this advertisement, we have stopped the custom of always quoting only the cheapest prices.... We want to remain true to our reputation, which has helped us achieve the title of honor of "The Quality Goods Department Store in Donaueschingen".[6]

---

[6] Announcement in *Donaueschingen Tagblatt* on November 25, 1932. Until now, Guggenheim, as well as its competitors, had mainly advertised its cheap, penny-priced articles.

On December 1, 1932, only a few weeks before the National Socialists (Nazis) regime takeover, Abraham Guggenheim died. He was buried in his hometown of Gailingen with great public participation and in the presence of almost the entire personnel of all three department stores.[7] The obituary that appeared a few days later in the local daily paper expressed the high esteem that the deceased had enjoyed among the residents due to his active charitable commitment and his generous granting of credit to his customers. Given this acknowledgement, it is difficult to fathom that only a few months later a number of customers, goaded by political leaders in Donaueschingen, radically changed their attitude toward the Guggenheims.

After the death of the company's director Abraham Guggenheim, his wife Bona continued to manage the stores in Donaueschingen as a co-partner.

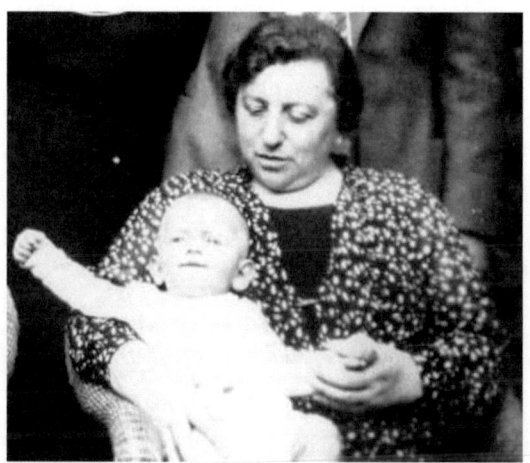

Bona Guggenheim with grandson Alfred 1933 (Photo courtesy of Beatriz Strauss)

Dagobert's professional development can be traced through his sister Erna's written statement for a reparation court case.[8] After completion of secondary education at the high school in Villingen, Dagobert began

---

[7] The Donaueschingen Jewish Community was part of the Gailingen Rabbinate District. It did not have its own cemetery. See Volkhard Huth, *Donaueschingen, Stadt am Ursprung der Donau* [City at the Source of the Danube] (Sigmaringen: Jan Thorbecke Publisher, 1989), p. 209.

[8] Affidavit statement of Erna Strauss on August 18, 1962. (State Archives Freiburg, File F196/1, Req. No. 5800).

commercial training with Alsberg & Co. in Bielefeld. He worked there for several years and then moved to Sonder & Co. in Leipzig. These training years consisted of rotating assignments and responsibilities in various commercial departments with the goal of co-managing his parents' business. With the death of his father at the beginning of December 1932, Dagobert's professional traveling years ended; his mother Bona called him back to support her in Donaueschingen, where he assumed the position of assistant to the business management.

After the Seizure of Power: Emigration or Waiting It Out

When Bona and son Dagobert took over the management of the Guggenheim department stores at the end of 1932, they could already see the dark clouds looming over the business sky of the Guggenheims and the other Jewish business owners. The increasingly aggressive Nazis made no secret of their penchant for boycotting Jewish businesses even before the seizure of power on January 30, 1933. On April 1, 1933, a thunderstorm crashed down on the Jewish business world with the Nazi regime's call for the national boycott of Jewish stores. In Donaueschingen, too, the local Nazis and the Nazi propaganda paper *Schwarzwälder Tagblatt* [Black Forest Daily Paper] agitated against the Jewish department stores and called for a boycott.

"No honest, conscientious German can continue to buy from a Jew...."[9] And further: *"Department stores, specialty stores and junk markets are the desecration of the entire German Volk (people)...."*[10]

It should be noted that the boycott measures were only minimally effective in Donaueschingen. The residents left the agitators virtually empty-handed by making their purchases the day before.[11]

But the local Nazi operatives left their odious anti-Semitic telltale scent on a conspicuous place: directly in front of the Donaueschingen City Hall. The very visible derogatory graffiti *"The Jews are our misfortune"* on the public newspaper dispensers must have caused great anxiety among the Guggenheims and other Donaueschingen Jews.

---

[9] *Schwarzwälder Tagblatt* [Black Forest Daily Paper], March 31, 1933.
[10] *Ibid.*, April 8, 1933.
[11] Volkhard Huth, *Donaueschingen...*, *op. cit.*, p. 196.

Anti-Semitic derogatory graffiti in Donaueschingen around 1933 (Photo source: Volkhard Huth, *Donaueschingen, Stadt am Ursprung der Donau* [City at the Source of the Danube])

Although the Donaueschingen citizens had just recently showered high regard and appreciation on the deceased Abraham Guggenheim, a World War I front soldier, the Nazi agitators' malicious campaign succeeded in socially ostracizing the Jews.

Since Hermann Einstein, the other co-founder of the Guggenheim Department Store, had already died in 1928, the two widows, Bona Guggenheim and Klara Einstein, made the following decisions in September 1933 that would give them more protection from business and personal risks. One was to move the head office of the business from Donaueschingen to Singen, where Emil Frank, a third shareholder, was operating the store; another was to officially make Emil Frank a third owner of the property.

The Herrmann and Klara Einstein family: (upper row from left), children Norbert, Trude and Leopold, Konstanz around 1910 (Photo source: Konstanz City Archives; see also *"Auf der Suche nach Norbert Einstein"* [Searching for Norbert Einstein] in: Norbert Einstein, *Der Alltag – Aufsätze zum Wesen der Gesellschaft* [Daily Life – Essays about the Nature of Society]. München, 1918, Zürich, 1978, p. 96ff.)

Subsequently, the Guggenheim Department Store with its broad-based advertising continued to have a strong presence at the Donaueschingen location. The living conditions for Jews, however, deteriorated drastically with the "Nuremberg Laws," enacted on September 15, 1935, during the Reich's Party Day in Nuremberg. As mere "state citizens," Jews now had an inferior status as opposed to "Aryans," who had special political rights as "Reich's (regime) citizens." The "Reich's Citizen Law" with its various yet-to-be-enforced regulations had the effect of systematically invalidating the cultural and social achievements of the Jews.

And yet Bona and Dagobert persevered in Donaueschingen, continuing to operate the business that had been built over many years with hard work and great commitment, hoping that the "brown spook" (the brown-uniformed SA) would not last all that long.

Daughter Erna, however, did not have that much patience. The increasing discrimination and lack of prospects led her to emigrate from Germany as the first member of the two Konstanz and Donaueschingen families. Erna had married the tailor Ludwig Strauss and moved to Frankfurt/Main. From there, the couple emigrated to Argentina with their son Alfred in 1935, who was born two years earlier. Their destination was Buenos Aires, the capital and thriving metropolis. They moved into an apartment on the Avenida la Plata in centrally located Caballito. With that move, Erna established the escape route and set an address of destination for other members for both Guggenheim families' future emigration attempts.

Erna and Ludwig Strauss, ca. 1933 (Photo courtesy of Beatriz Strauss)

At that time, emigration was still relatively unproblematic, because the Latin American countries, especially those in the south (Argentina, Brazil, Chile, Uruguay), were taking in large numbers of immigrants from Europe. And the Nazi dictators – in this case, the Gestapo and SS (*Schutzstaffel* [State Security]) – and not the SA (*Sturmabteilung* [Storm Detachment])! – even encouraged an "orderly" state police-sanctioned emigration of Jewish citizens. In this ingenious way, they could "catch two birds with one stone": For one thing, the emigrants helped them by "voluntarily" fulfilling the task of making Germany *judenrein* [free of Jews]; and for another, the emigrants' property – forcibly left behind – automatically went to the regime with the expatriation.

For the Konstanz Guggenheims, the political changes since 1933 had an increasingly detrimental effect on the already strained financial situation of the parents Salomon and Toni. After Salomon had to give up his own business resulting from the Great Depression at the beginning of the 1930s, he was earning the family's livelihood as a commission agent for machines and tools, although at a sharply reduced income. With the 1935 enacted "Nuremberg Laws," Salomon, like all other working Jews, was so restricted in his professional practice that his income amounted to zero.[12] The salary earned by son Isi, who had just entered his professional career as an employee of the Hermann Einstein clothing store, was not able to support the communal household, as the monthly rent alone came to 64 Reichsmarks (RM). Just as for many Jewish citizens still in Germany, the "Nuremberg Laws" signified for the Guggenheims the onset of social decline over many years and, eventually, actual annihilation.

Under these difficult circumstances, the Konstanz Guggenheims were cushioned by a financial net that had been forged by the Donaueschingen relatives. Bona, the "good one" as the name suggests, lived up to her name by supporting the family of her sister Toni, 10 years her junior, with regular financial contributions. This assistance enabled her sister and brother-in-law in Konstanz to maintain for the time being a secure livelihood and residence in the four-room apartment on Hüetlinstraße. Because of this, despite the increasing discrimination, the Konstanz Guggenheims did not have plans to leave the country at that time. They were hoping for a political change with a

---

[12] Salomon Guggenheim's annual income declared for tax purposes in 1936 to 1938 ranged from 99 to 182 RM (documented by Salomon Guggenheim for the Konstanz Finance Office on March 9, 1939). (See: Freiburg State Archives, File F 196/1, No. 10031.)

return to better times for the Jewish population. For this survival strategy to work, however, they had to be completely inconspicuous in public.[13]

The Rosenwalds of Cologne

Many Jewish families had such anxieties – the same or similar extent – about their existence at this time, among them the Rosenwald family of four of Cologne. The son, Fritz, was the link to the connection of his Cologne-based family with the Guggenheims of Konstanz and later, with the Donaueschingen Guggenheims. The Rosenwald family was made up of the parents Karl and Johanna, née Ledermann, and the children Lisel and Fritz. The fates of family members show the remarkable intersections and parallels with the individual Guggenheims. The connection with the Cologne Rosenwalds was established with the Guggenheims of Konstanz and Donaueschingen in the mid-1930s. Though the available documents give no clue as to how and when the Guggenheims and Rosenwalds first met, it is known that as of 1935 or 1936, Fritz Rosenwald established a close relationship with Isi, the son of the Konstanz Guggenheims.

They met in Konstanz. Fritz Rosenwald, born in May 1915 and just a few days younger than Isi Guggenheim, had moved from Cologne to Konstanz, where he had found a position as a commercial employee with the company Schweizer Lohnstickerei. The owner of the company based in the Konstanz Raueneckgasse was the Jewish entrepreneur Moritz Rosenthal. The relatively liberal atmosphere of the Konstanz – the city bordering on Switzerland – made life much more tolerable than in the big cities of the interior; this played an important role in Fritz's move from Cologne to Konstanz, as it did for many other Jewish people settling there. It is assumed that Fritz was shunned or even reviled in his hometown because of his dark skin tone and his foreign appearance.[14] Fritz moved several times during his three-year stay there, though he lived at Franz Seldte-Straße 30 (today Schützenstraße) most of the time.

It may have been the shared professional interest in the textile trade that brought the two young men Isi Guggenheim and Fritz Rosenwald together; more likely, though, the basis of their close friendship was a mutual affinity.

---

[13] In all the available sources, the author was unable to find any clues about the activities of the Guggenheims in the business life or leadership positions in the Konstanz Jewish Community.

[14] Assumption of daughter Joan Rosenwald-Fradkin, letter of February 3, 2019 to the author.

For Fritz, the newcomer to Konstanz, it must have been very helpful that Isi supported him with getting settled in and becoming familiar with the peculiarities of the Lake Konstanz area's unique way of life.

That Fritz Rosenwald has some attractive qualities is demonstrated by the fact that he was also heartily welcomed by Isi's parents. There are photos showing Fritz as Salomon and Toni Guggenheim's guest in their residence at Hüetlinstraße 21.

Fritz Rosenwald as guest of the Salomon Guggenheim family in the Konstanz Hüetlinstraße, Toni Guggenheim in the background, taken in the mid-1930s (Photo courtesy of Joan Fradkin)

Isi Guggenheim and Fritz Rosenwald, taken in the mid-1930s (Photo courtesy of Joan Fradkin)

In their free time, the friends – both handsome and elegantly dressed – used every opportunity for social interaction still available to them in the Nazi regime's ever increasing restrictions against Jewish citizens. Though their access to most games, sports and entertainment venues was limited, these two fun-loving young men took excursions around the beautiful Lake Konstanz area, as well as trips to friends and relatives in Zurich and Lucerne in Switzerland – sometimes even in the company of young ladies.[15]

Lisel Rosenwald – July 1939 (Photo courtesy of Joan Fradkin)

One of these young women was Lisel Rosenwald, Fritz's sister, older by one year. The two siblings were very close, whereby the sister also had certain protective feelings toward her brother.[16] So it was natural – perhaps also at the wish of her parents – that Lisel wanted to see how her brother was doing, now that he was on his own. Aside from that, this lively young woman may have been drawn to the tourist magnet, Konstanz, on the

---

[15] Proof of this can be found in the extensive collection of letters that Fritz Rosenwald later in the USA received and saved from his family members remaining in Germany. They are made accessible in the internet by Joan Fradkin, at https://collections.ushmm.org/search/catalog/im73437. *(Rosenwald family papers-Collections Search-United States.*

[16] This quality becomes very clear in later letters Lisel sends her brother in the USA from 1938 to 1941; *see Rosenwald family papers, op. cit.*

beautiful lake of the same name. The photos taken during her visit there show that she felt quite happy to be in the company of young men.

Trip to Mainau Island – friends Lisel Rosenwald and Dagobert Guggenheim (foreground), behind them from left, Isi Guggenheim and Fritz Rosenwald (Photo source: Joan Fradkin)

Enlarging this circle of friends was Dagobert Guggenheim, Isi's cousin, during one of his visits to the Konstanz relatives. "Dago", as he was called, soon developed a strong affection for the attractive Lisel. From letters written by mother Johanna and sister Lisel as of 1938 to Fritz Rosenwald, it is clear that Lisel did not initially respond in the same way to Dago's feelings. She did appreciate the generosity he showed with invitations and presents for her and her parents. One time, she was happy about some fabric from which she could make a stylish dress.[17] Another time, mother Johanna

---

[17] *Rosenwald family papers, Correspondence Karl, Johanna, ... May 3 1938, item 15.*

received a scarf and a large bottle of Eau de Cologne.[18] But this young woman with a tendency to the finer things in life, was not ready to begin a closer relationship with the somewhat corpulent[19] and seemingly shy Dago, much to the regret of her mother.[20] Lisel, who worked as a milliner, was much more fun-loving than Dago, being mostly interested in fashion and dancing. She asked her brother several times to let her know what fashion trends she should emulate from New York, if she – as she was planning to do – were soon to follow this brother, who had managed to emigrate there.[21]

At the same time, a relationship developed between Lisel and Dago that was to grow more serious with time, as the living conditions of the Jewish population gradually deteriorated. For the time being, they remained in contact. Experience shows that in situations of threat and great need, affected groups form closer bonds. And friendship can blossom into love.

Lisel and Dago stayed connected with letters between Cologne and Donaueschingen, and later Konstanz. Face-to-face connections came with Dagobert's visit to Cologne, as well as occasional meetings in other places, like Frankfurt and Karlsruhe. Dago had fond memories of his stay in Cologne at the beginning of 1939 because of the social and entertainment opportunities.[22] But, for the time being, there were no prospects for a future together. Both of them continued to pursue emigration – as in the case of Isi and Fritz – but with different destinations. Lisel wanted to join her brother Fritz in the USA. She was assigned the preregistration No. 12,770 by the American Consulate in Stuttgart.[23] Dago, on the other hand, tried – with mother Bona – to emigrate to Argentina through his connection with his sister and her family there. Lisel and Dago took it for granted, that they would lose contact with each other then.

Friends Isi and Fritz emigrate from Germany

In 1938, yet another member of the Guggenheim family's younger generation turned his back on Germany. As one of the last of the so-called emigration wave – later to be replaced by mass flight after the November

---

[18] *Rosenwald family papers, op. cit., Jan. 30 1939, item 7.*
[19] Within the family, Lisel jokingly called Dago "the fat one".
[20] Ebenda
[21] Correspondence ... 1938, letter Lisel R. of February 8, 1938, item 15.
[22] Correspondence ... 1939, letter of January 30, 1939, item 6.
[23] Letter of Lisel R. to her brother Fritz on August 24, 1938, correspondence ... 1938, item 21.

Pogrom (also known as *Kristallnacht*) in 1938 – 23-year old Isi also emigrated to Argentina. He used the address and the local connection needed for entry papers provided by his cousin Erna and her husband Ludwig Strauss who lived in Buenos Aires for three years as his base. The expenses of the trip on the ocean liner *Jamaique* amounting to 5,000 RM were again covered from Bona Guggenheim's property in Donaueschingen.[24] A large part of these costs was due to the sharply increased visa fees as of 1931.

Of course, the ostracism and repression that impeded prospects in the lives of young Jews played a role in Isi's leaving his parents and homeland. Added to that was the knowledge that some very good friends with whom he had gone to school and professional training had left Germany one by one. Isi met some of them later in Buenos Aires – the old classmates Kurt Löwenstein and Kurt Thanhauser, who had already emigrated in 1936 and 1937, either directly or via detours to South America.

Isi Guggenheim with an unnamed woman, Konstanz mid-1930s (Photo source: Joan Fradkin)

It may also be assumed that a big disappointment in Isi's emotional life made it easier for him to leave Germany. The relationship with a Gentile

---

[24] Salomon Guggenheim's declaration on file with the Konstanz Finance Office. *See:* footnote 12

young woman was ended by her; she was not able to stand up to the pressure of her family.[25] Isi quit his position with the Hermann Einstein Company in April 1938. The administration wished him success for his plans "to find a new sphere of activity" and sent him off on his journey with the highest recommendations.[26]

Yet the determining factor for the emigration was surely the lack of prospects available to the two young, ambitious Jewish men because of the current political and social climate. Isi Guggenheim and Fritz Rosenwald were at an age of professional development. It can therefore be assumed that as of 1937 – at the latest – both had made arrangements and mutual preparations for an imminent emigration to countries with promising opportunities and a life of safety.

With the decision to emigrate at the same time came the realization that their paths would separate – at least for a long time. While Isi wanted to emigrate to South America, Fritz had chosen North America – New York City – as his destination. A great-aunt living there had submitted the required guarantee for his entry.

Two months before Isi's departure, Fritz left Hamburg on the steamship *Manhattan* at the beginning of March 1938, arriving in New York on March 18. He obtained a position there with the well-known textile retail chain S. Klein.

As it turned out, Isi and Fritz had taken advantage of a favorable window of time with their emigration in the spring of 1938. Only a short time later – in July 1938 – the efforts of the key host countries failed at the French Evian Conference in setting higher allotments for accepting Jews from Germany and the recently "annexed" Austria to the German Reich. Although the number of those wanting to emigrate had markedly increased since March 1938 through the inclusion of Austrian Jews, even the USA was not willing to raise its annual quota of 27,270 Jewish immigrants.[27] Because the quota remained the same but the Austrian Jews wanting to emigrate increased, the chances for an entry visa to the USA had diminished for the applicants from the "Greater German Reich" as of mid-1938. The other host countries, too –

---

[25] Written statement of Gabriela Guggenheim (Isi's daughter) residing in Buenos Aires, April 8, 2008, H.H. Seiffert archive.

[26] Performance evaluation of the Hermann Einstein Company of April 19, 1938 (Gabriela Guggenheim private archive).

[27] Declaration of the U.S. conference leader Myron Taylor in his opening remarks on July 6, 1938, quoted by Thomas Schmid, Susanne Heim, *Wir sind kein Einwanderungsland, Konferenz von Évian 1938, [We are not an Immigration Country, Évian Conference 1938]*, DIE ZEIT, No. 28/1998.

Argentina among them – resorted to restrictive measures for Jewish refugees from Europe.

Lisel Rosenwald and Dagobert Guggenheim, as well as Isi's parents, would run up against this very situation later.

Hermann Einstein M/H.   KONSTANZ, den

Fernsprecher Nr. 290
Postscheckkonto 2202
Karlsruhe

Z e u g n i s .

Herr Isi G u g g e n h e i m aus Konstanz trat bei
uns am 1. April 1931 als Lehrling ein und beendete seine
kaufmännische Lehre am 1. April 1934. Während dieser
dreijährigen Lehrzeit zeigte Herr Guggenheim regen
Fleiss, gute Auffassungsgabe und grosses Geschäftsin-
teresse.

Er eignete sich gute grundlegende Warenkenntnisse an
und entwickelte sich zu einem gewandten Verkäufer. –
Vornehmlich wurde Herr Guggenheim als Lagerist beschäf-
tigt; in dieser Eigenschaft erledigte er den gesamten
Wareneingang und die Waren – Kalkulation mit grosser
Pünktlichkeit und Selbständigkeit.

Nach Beendigung seiner Lehre wurde Herr Guggenheim bei
uns bis heute weiter beschäftigt und zwar als Verkäufer
und Substitut, d.h. zur persönlichen Unterstützung der
Geschäftsleitung, sodass er auch im Wareneinkauf inten-
siv herangezogen wurde, da er auch hierfür die notwen-
digen Kenntnisse zeigte.

Es sei weiter erwähnt, dass Herr Guggenheim aushilfsweise
auch in der Buchhaltung und Statistik beschäftigt wurde.

Alles in Allem bestätigen wir, dass Herr Guggenheim
sich zu einem sehr brauchbaren und rührigen jungen
Kaufmann entwickelt hat; er ist durchaus ehrlich,
treu und von verträglichem Charakter. Wegen Krankheit
hat er nur ganz selten gefehlt.

Herr Guggenheim verlässt seine Stellung bei uns auf
eigenen Wunsch, da er sich im Ausland einen neuen
Wirkungskreis suchen will. Wir bedauern seinen Weggang
sehr und wünschen ihm für seine Zukunft das Beste !

Wir können Herrn Guggenheim jederzeit bestens empfehlen.

Konstanz, den 19. April 1938.

Hermann Einstein
Konstanz

Performance evaluation of the Hermann Einstein Company for Isi Guggenheim (Photo courtesy of Gabriela Guggenheim)

Translation:
Hermann Einstein   M-H.   Konstanz
Phone No. 290
Postal Bank Account 2202
Karlsruhe

Performance Evaluation

Mr. Isi Guggenheim of Konstanz started with us as an apprentice on April 1, 1931, and completed his commercial apprenticeship on April 1, 1934. During this three-year apprenticeship, Mr. Guggenheim showed great diligence, good comprehension and a great interest in the business.

He acquired a good basic knowledge of products and developed into a skilled salesman. Mr. Guggenheim was mainly employed as a warehouse clerk; in this position, he took care of all incoming goods and product calculation with great punctuality and self-reliance.

Upon completion of his apprenticeship, Mr. Guggenheim continued to work for us as a salesman and substitute, that is, as personal support to the company administration, and he helped a great deal with the purchase of goods, as he showed the necessary knowledge in this area as well.

In addition, it should be noted that Mr. Guggenheim developed into a very useful and enterprising young businessman; he is completely honest, loyal and with an exemplary character. He rarely took a sick day.

Mr. Guggenheim is leaving his position with us on his own accord, as he intends to find a new sphere of activity abroad. We very much regret his departure and wish him all the best for his future!

We stand ready to recommend Mr. Guggenheim highly at any time.

Konstanz, April 19, 1938.

Hermann Einstein
Konstanz
Signature

Safe Haven Argentina as Refuge from Nazi Germany

Why had the members of the two Guggenheim families chosen Argentina as their emigration destination?

In the case of Isi, who emigrated later, it is clear that the much-needed address of cousin Erna played a major role. The support of family members was one of the preconditions of host countries to grant entry permits. On the other hand, Erna Strauss's family, having immigrated three years earlier, based their choice of Argentina on the relatively favorable conditions for entry at that time and for life in exile.

Buenos Aires, Avenida 9 de Julio, in the 1940s (Postcard source: H.-H. Seiffert)

That is how many Jews of Baden-Württemberg thought and acted as well. Thus, roughly 800 Jews fled from southwest Germany to Argentina during the time of the Nazi persecution.[28] Argentina was second only to the USA in accepting the largest number of Jewish refugees from Germany. There was a special attraction about the Argentine asylum landscape, unique in Latin America, which developed into a small "German cosmos."[29] Compared to Chile or southern Brazil where German immigrants spread out across the broad, thinly settled areas, the German population of Argentina concentrated itself mostly in the capital city of Buenos Aires. Estimates suggest a minimum of 35,000 Germans and ethnic Germans.[30]

The focus in the choice of residence fostered a tight and strong development of the political, cultural and religious infrastructure. This meant that in Buenos Aires alone there were many German schools and hundreds of German clubs, as well as a number of church and synagogue

[28] Paul Sauer, *Die Schicksale der jüdischen Bürger Baden-Württembergs während der nationalistischen Verfolgungszeit 1933-1945* [The Fate of Jewish Baden-Württemberg's Citizens During the Nazi Time of Persecution 1933-1945] (Stuttgart: 1969), p. 233.
[29] Patrik von zur Mühlen, *Fluchtziel Lateinamerika, Die deutsche Emigration 1933-1945* [Safe Haven Latin America, German Emigration 1933-1945] (Bonn: 1988), p. 136.
[30] Von zur Mühlen, *op. cit.*, p. 140.

communities. Among them were groups of opposing political views that were not necessarily friendly with one another. On the one hand, this included a largely unified foreign and ethnic German colony from which the local branch of the Nazis was recruited. On the other were liberal and left-leaning organizations, newspapers and schools offering the emigrants shelter and support.

The "Benevolent Society of German-speaking Jews" had been established in 1933 to care for the Jews fleeing Germany and support them financially to the best of its ability.[31]

After a four-week ship's passage from Le Havre, France, Isi Guggenheim immersed himself in this German "cosmos" upon arriving in Buenos Aires on June 2, 1938. He was able to negotiate the immigration to Argentina just in time, before a short time later when the acceptance of German Jews was made more difficult with the Argentine government decrees in July and August 1938. From then on, acceptance of immigrants was decided mostly on the basis of professional qualifications. Thereafter, skills in agricultural training and practice were especially favored. Isi, however, was able to begin his new professional life in the business sector familiar to him: Initially, he was a commissions agent for a company in the food industry and later as a distributor of packaging.

The Guggenheim Families at the Mercy of the Nazi Dictatorship in 1938

At the same time as the end of his relationship with the Gentile woman – as a result of the state-decreed discrimination against Jews – that drove Isi Guggenheim to emigrate, the pressure of the Nazi dictatorship also increased for businesswoman Bona Guggenheim. Like many other Jewish businesspeople, she was forced to sell her part of the business, according to the terminology back then, to "an honest, German businessman."

To get an overview of the size and value of Jewish assets, the Reich government passed a decree on April 23, 1938 by which all Jewish citizens of the German Reich were required to register their assets if they were worth more than 5,000 Reichsmarks.[32] This regulation prepared the way for the ensuing expropriation of Jewish properties with which economic influence could be exercised.

---

[31] Sauer, *op. cit.*, p. 235.
[32] *Reichsgesetzblatt I.* [Reich's Law Gazette I.], p. 414ff.

The expropriation of the Guggenheim department store was carried out in all three branches during the same year. The Gaggenau branch had already closed its doors on February 28, 1938. The neo-classical commercial building, which the Guggenheim company had been renting since 1912, was taken over by the Bracht clothing store, which also bought parts of the Guggenheim warehouse.[33]

At the end of September 1938, the Muck & Co. business, represented by the owners Muck & Schuler, took over the Guggenheim business in Singen. At the beginning of January 1939, the businessman Schuler bought the building there for a "bargain price," amounting to about half of the true market value.[34]

In Donaueschingen, the business activities and the influence the Guggenheim family had on the business climate ended almost at the same time as in Singen. Effective October 1, 1938, the Guggenheim department store on Max-Egon-Straße and the building on Wasserstraße were forcibly sold to the mineral water manufacturer Anton Volk and his wife. The recording of the property's sales contract, as well as the store's inventory, was completed on August 31, 1938.[35] The proceeds of the sale were distributed among the three owners: the Guggenheim, Einstein and Frank families. But the former owners could not dispose of these revenues without restrictions: Their bank accounts had been closed, so that in case of emigration, the "Reich's escape tax" of 25 percent of total assets, could be taken from them. With this tax, the "creative" Reich's Finance Ministry had devised a special method of quasi-legally plundering Jewish assets.

The liquidation of Guggenheim & Cie. was completed with the entry into the Commercial Registry on December 20, 1938. The businessman Willi Schuler of Konstanz took over the business as lessee of the property on Max-Egon-Straße. The business equipment and warehouse were sold to him. Following the reopening on October 8, 1938, he lauded his store as being "in new, Aryan hands."[36]

Bona and son Dagobert were allowed to stay in their residence until April 1939 – rent free till the end of October 1938, but then at a monthly rental of 100 RM.

---

[33] Letter from the Gaggenau City Archive to the author, July 2, 2009.
[34] Kappes, *op. cit.*, p. 35.
[35] Written disclosure of the Donaueschingen City Archives, March 2, 2009.
[36] *Schwarzwälder Tagblatt*, October 7, 1938.

Announcement in the *Schwarzwälder Tagblatt* [Black Forest Daily Paper], October 7, 1938

Translation:
Reopening
The former company
Guggenheim & Co. Donaueschingen
is now in new, Aryan hands
Large assortments in all departments
at the familiar favorable prices
It will always be my intention
To give good advice and serve you with reasonable prices
Willi Schuler
Donaueschingen
The department store for everyone

The two Guggenheims availed themselves of their residential rights in their former building for only a few weeks. During the *Reichspogromnacht*, November 9–10, 1938, the four Jewish families still living in Donaueschingen became easy and completely helpless victims of the acts of terror unleashed by fanatic Nazi supporters. Among them were many students who were incited and goaded[37] by SA people[38] in civilian clothes.

Bona and Dagobert had to watch as a mob smeared their building with anti-Semitic graffiti, went on a rampage and eventually burst into the apartment, destroying the furniture. Even worse was the threat of bodily harm. An eye witness seeing the action in the Guggenheim building later reported:

At the Guggenheims' building, it was possible to go into the store. I went in on the hallway side because I used to be there frequently to pick up old food for the pigs. Upon entering, I heard banging, screaming. I looked up the stairs and saw Guggenheim covered in blood and a woman being pulled back and forth by her hair.[39]

The traumatic effects that the events of November 10 had on Bona Guggenheim are found in a certified report of the mayor and a neighbor, a document she added to her restitution application in October 1950 with the District Office for Restitution in Freiburg:[40]

On the day of the arrest [of son Dagobert on November 10 – Ed.], the SA and SS forced their way into my residence in Donaueschingen and smashed everything to smithereens. The dining room, bedrooms, study and kitchen were all demolished. The shattered items were then thrown out of the window onto the street. Highly valuable crystal items, oil paintings, porcelain, 1 Leica camera, jewelry, three gold wristwatches..., lamps, dinner and coffee sets, all were destroyed or stolen. As a result of the shock and bedlam of this pogrom, I lost my hearing.

---

[37] See Huth, *Donaueschingen...*, *op. cit.*, p. 210.

[38] The initials SA stand for *Sturmabteilung* [Storm Detachment]. The SA was a paramilitary service of the NSDAP, National Socialist German Workers Party, which among other activities, was involved in violent confrontations with political opponents.

[39] Description of the former altar boy Herbert Bayer, in: Richard Zahlten, "Dr. Heinrich Feurstein," *Donaueschingen 1992*, p. 111.

[40] Freiburg State Archives, File F 196/1, EF 5800.

Anti-Semitic graffiti on the Guggenheim department store, Donaueschingen, November 9 and 10, 1938 (Photo source: Donaueschingen City Archives)

The next day, November 11, 1938, 28-year old Dagobert was arrested by the Gestapo[41] and taken to the Dachau concentration camp. With prisoner number 22 489, he remained there until December 20, 1938 in "protective custody" – a ludicrous metaphor for an action that provided everything but protection from the persecutors. With this action, he shared the fate of many other Jewish men taken into "protective custody" by the Nazi regime following the assassination of the diplomat Ernst vom Rath by the Jewish man, Herschel Grynszpan, in Paris a few days before.

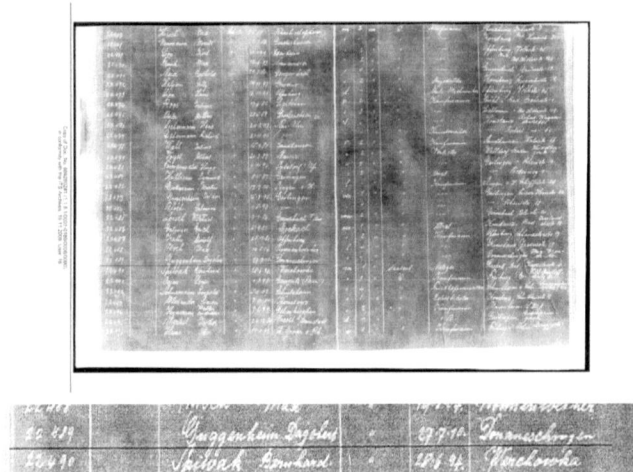

Excerpt from the registration book of the Dachau concentration camp (Photo source: International Tracing Service, Arolsen)

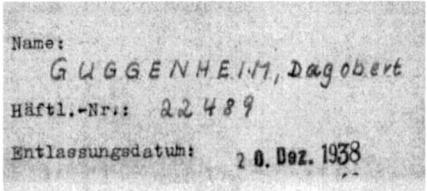

Discharge registration from the Dachau concentration camp (Photo source: ITS Arolsen)

---

[41] *Geheime Staatspolizei* [Secret State Police] (Department IV of the Reich's Security Headquarters, the RSHA).

The *Reichskristallnacht* ["Night of the Broken Glass"] of November 9 and 10 signified yet another chasm and new dimension of organized terror: The discrimination and ostracism of the Jews had now become targeted persecution.

In Cologne, Lisel Rosenwald and her parents were not affected by the effects of Pogrom Night to the same extent as the Guggenheims of Donaueschingen. As non-business owners they were not in a particularly vulnerable position in a big city like Cologne.

There is no doubt, however, that the rioting against the Jewish people, the plundering and destruction of Jewish property, must have driven fear into the Rosenwalds as well. Only in a hedging way – because of the suspected censorship of correspondence going abroad – Lisel writes her brother in a letter about the November 10 events:

"You don't need to worry about us, we are in good health, that is the main thing. You will know more than we do."

At the same time, she expresses her hope that the host countries will increase their quotas for Jews from Germany.[42]

Since Pogrom Night, Lisel had the inescapable feeling that life for Jews remaining in Germany was getting increasingly dangerous. She asked her brother in the "safe haven" of New York to step up his efforts for her entry visa.

Lisel had heard about Dago's "protective" custody in Dachau from his mother Bona. Toward the end of 1938, Lisel was able to send her brother the news that Dago had sent a telegram on December 22 upon being freed from Dachau.[43]

A Search for Safety Within Konstanz Family Connections

After November 10, Bona Guggenheim made an immediate decision to leave the site of the terrible assaults. As a prominent Jewish businesswoman, she had to expect more trouble and harassment by the local party supporters in Donaueschingen's highly charged atmosphere. Since Dagobert's arrest, she was also without any protection in the building. Bona's fears were

---

[42] Correspondence ... 1938, letter of November 10, 1938, item 48.
[43] Correspondence ... 1938, letter of December 12, 1938, item 45.

confirmed by the propaganda in the Nazi newspaper *Schwarzwälder Tagblatt* [Black Forest Daily News], which stated:

Donaueschingen's residents expect no Jew to remain within the walls of our city.[44]

On November 21, 1938, Bona moved in with her sister Toni and brother-in-law Salomon on Hüetlinstraße 21 in Konstanz and officially registered herself at this new residence on December 8, 1938. Here, in the lap of a larger Jewish congregation and the close-knit communal residence of her relatives, she hoped to live with more anonymity and less hostility.

After his release from Dachau, Dagobert went straight to his relatives in Konstanz and registered his residence at Hüetlinstraße 21 on December 22, 1938. As shown in a photo published by Erich Bloch,[45] he was soon accepted into a circle of Jewish male friends in Konstanz. From a letter written by Lisel to brother Fritz almost two years later, it is known that Dagobert was sent to forced labor in a brickyard located in Konstanz.[46] Not known, however, is the date on which he began his work at the brickyard.

One of his workmates was the two years older Hugo Schriesheimer, who would be deported with him, but who survived the Holocaust through a set of fortunate circumstances. (See chapter „Condemned to Waiting and Hoping")

Dagobert Guggenheim (second on right in background) among a circle of friends shortly before the deportation to Gurs in the fall of 1940. From left: Albert Spiegel, Siegfried Rothschild, Willy Rosenfeld, Ernst Hilb, Hugo Schriesheimer, Kurt Wolf (Photo source: Erich Bloch's estate, Konstanz City Archives)

---

[44] Cited in the *Badische Zeitung* [Badische Newspaper], November 10, 1992.
[45] Erich Bloch, *Geschichte der Juden von Konstanz* [The Story of the Jews of Konstanz] (Konstanz: 1971), p. 174.
[46] Correspondence … 1940, op. cit. Letter of Lisel R. of September 15, 1940, item 101.

Along with his Aunt Toni and Uncle Salomon, Dagobert would now build a close community with those who shared a similar fate; they would remain together until their deportation to Auschwitz. Both families benefited from his moving in with relatives. The impoverished couple Toni and Salomon received financial aid through Bona's disposable assets, while Bona and Dagobert, now in Konstanz, had gained some distance from the suffering they had endured in Donaueschingen.

Just as with the Lisel Rosenwald in Cologne after Pogrom Night, impatience grew among the four Guggenheims in Konstance to leave Germany for Argentina as quickly as possible. It had become clear to them that they could no longer live the lives they wanted amid the escalating anti-Semitism. With the November pogroms, the persecution had taken on a scope that left virtually no alternative to emigration. They sought shelter and security outside of Germany – amidst their relatives, who had already settled in the Argentina's capital city, Buenos Aires.

Emigration Attemps with Varying Degrees of Success

At the beginning of 1939, they undertook the first bureaucratic steps for emigration. On February 6, 1939, Salomon Guggenheim sent a request to the Baden Finance Office (the Currency Office) for taking possessions and luggage – listed in detail – for emigration to Argentina. And again, all expenses for the emigration, as well as the travel tickets and the "Dego" tax[47] were paid by sister-in-law Bona. A few weeks later on March 15, 1939, the Finance Office administration issued the document of taxable compliance as requested by the Currency Office. By granting a passport, the Konstanz district office obtained the compliance of other agencies at the same time. These included the customs investigation department in Radolfzell, the Reich's bank branch, the state police, the city rental office and the main tax office in Konstanz.

Bona submitted her application for emigration to Argentina at the same time as her brother-in-law. For her, the Konstanz Finance Office on February 24, 1939 calculated a Reich's escape tax of 19,675 RM. When Bona received her travel approval, she made the necessary preparations. On

---

[47] A tax, which had to paid upon emigration to the *Deutsche Golddiskontbank* [German Gold Discount Bank]. At the beginning that amounted to 90 percent of the transferred value.

March 27, 1939, the Carl Lassen moving company sent an invoice of 2,600 RM for moving costs.

Another eight months would pass until her departure. Among the likely reasons for the delay are the German agencies' time-consuming examination and approval procedures, as well as the difficulty in booking a steamship passage. The multitude of fiscal and administrative measures to be fulfilled by those who wanted to emigrate make the paradox clear: According to its race ideology, the Nazi regime had a strong interest in the emigration of its Jewish citizens; yet with its procedures and laws, it was effectively doing everything possible to make emigration difficult.

In the case of Bona's emigration, however, the delay had a different reason. Though she did need some time for confirmation of her ship ticket after receiving her entry visa, the most important hold-up of her emigration was the fact that this caring mother did not want to leave without her son Dagobert.[48] She was worried about him – after his imprisonment in Dachau, he had become ill with a boil on his arm.[49]

Jewish emigrants in Bremerhaven 1938 – Farewell without a greeting (Photo source: W. Rügert, ed., *Jüdisches Leben in Konstanz* [Jewish Life in Konstanz])

---

[48] As written by Lisel to her brother Fritz: "His mother *(Bona)* could be long gone, but she wants to wait to see what Dago will do." Correspondence ... 1939, letter of May 4, 1939, item 60.

[49] Correspondence by Lisel to Fritz ... 1939, letter of February 1, 1939, item 10.

On September 1, 1939, World War II began. Bona was finally able to leave Germany on December 4, 1939, with a cash amount of 10 RM. The entire remaining assets fell into the hands of the German Reich. Just before that she was still able to pay 185 dollars for the voyage. The passage to Argentina went from Genoa on the steamship *Oceania*, a liner taking various passengers to Central and South America with mostly Jewish immigrants. Upon arriving in Buenos Aires, Bona was taken in by her daughter Erna Strauss. As described in other parts of this book, until her departure Bona still had to live through some hardships with forced relocations in Konstanz – one last form of harassment by the Nazi dictatorship.

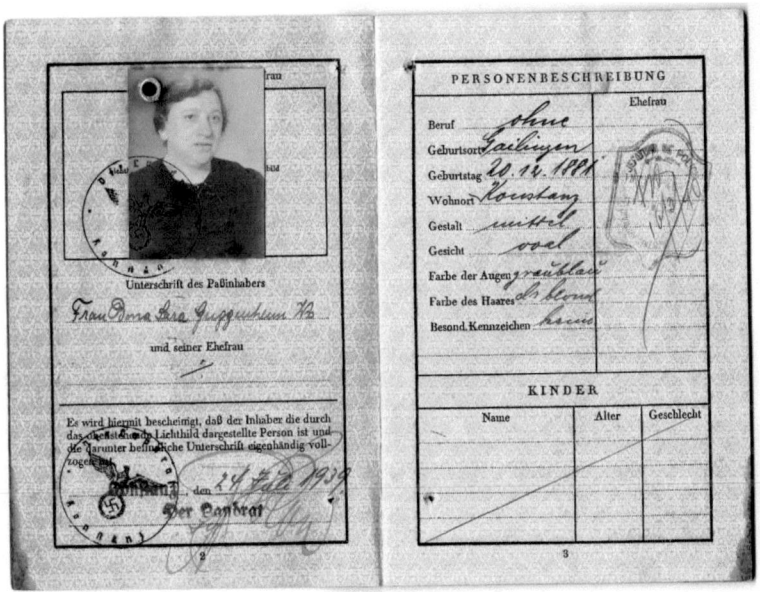

Bona Guggenheim's new passport for her emigration to Argentina issued July 1939
(Photo courtesy of Beatriz Strauss Archive)

It turned out that Bona was the last member of the family clan who succeeded in escaping the Nazi terror. The applicants Toni, Salomon and Dagobert Guggenheim were put to a hard test. The increasing flood of emigration applications caused by *Pogromnacht* [Pogrom Night] led to the overseas host countries putting restrictive entry policies into practice. This was particularly the case with Argentina, which, after the USA, was the second most important host country. Especially after 1940, when the archconservative and Nazi-friendly Vice President Ramon Castillo took over the government forces from the ailing President Roberto Ortiz – who supported the Allies – the chances of immigration for Jewish refugees clearly decreased.

During this time, Dago tried to organize emigration to other South American countries. Lisel, who was in regular contact with him and occasionally met with him, reported that Dago "has papers for Paraguay".[50] But that must have been only about application forms. The possibility of Paraguay is no longer mentioned after this. A bit later, she facetiously writes about Dago's obvious misjudgment of the actual situation:

"The fat one has been emigrating for a year now and this thing is not going any further because Argentina is closed. I talk about something only when it is imminent and not months before.[51]

Now the three Guggenheims in Konstanz changed their emigration destination and applied for departure to Chile, with a transit visa for continuing to Argentina. This made sense because between May and August 1939 the Chilean government had temporarily loosened its strict immigration conditions and granted entry to several thousand Jews from Germany and Austria.[52]

The three Guggenheims now hoped to benefit from this opening. Their joint application was "registered" at the Chilean Consulate in Bremen with the number 1,301.[53] Expecting to receive their entry permits very soon, they had already found a buyer for their apartment furniture and arranged its transfer to him upon their departure.

---

[50] Correspondence ... 1939, letter of February 17, 1939, item 23.
[51] Correspondence ... 1939, letter of February 26, 1939, item 27.
[52] Sauer, *op.cit.,* p. 240.
[53] Memorandum of the Konstanz Housing Office of July 26, 1939, after a summons of Dagobert Guggenheim. Source: Konstanz City Archives, File *Gesetz über Mietverhältnisse mit Juden* [Law pertaining to Leases with Jews].

Chaotic Search for Residence in Konstanz, 1939

At the same time that Bona and the other three Guggenheims were making their departure preparations, they were confronted with an unpleasant surprise. With the "Law Pertaining to Leases with Jews," the Reich regime on April 30, 1939 had created a quasi-legal basis for denying Jews protection against wrongful eviction from rental property, another act of disfranchisement. Now almost all Jews renting in buildings of "Aryan" owners received an eviction notice, provided they were offered a place with a Jewish landlord. This led to a concentration of Jewish residences in so-called "Jewish houses" – clearly intended as such.

The Guggenheims were immediately affected by this law, as the owner of the building on Hüetlinstraße 21 was the artist Hermann Apel residing in Berlin. The Konstanz resident, Willy Fischer of Saarlandstraße 16, acted as caretaker. The Guggenheims' lease had been in effect since 1913.

Toni Guggenheim in front of the building on Hüetlinstraße 21 at the end of the 1930s
(Photo courtesy of Gabriela Guggenheim)

From the documents of the Konstanz Housing Office regarding the law of April 30, 1939, it is evident that Salomon terminated the lease of the apartment on Hüetlinstraße 21 on August 1, 1939, effective September 1,

1939. He stated that he thought he could find quarters in the building belonging to the Jewish Culture Federation on Sigismundstraße 21 for himself and his family.[54]

Power of attorney statement by Salomon Guggenheim for Dagobert regarding a change of residence (Photo source: Konstanz City Archives, File *Gesetz über Mietverhältnisse ...* [Law Pertaining to Leases ...])

Translation of the above:
I hereby authorize my nephew Dagobert Israel Guggenheim to represent me in my summons with regard to the "Law Pertaining to Leases with Jews" next Wednesday, July 26, 1939, at 11 a.m. in the Römerstraße 13, as I will not be here at that time.

The question remains whether the termination was indeed made voluntarily; it is possible that the prospect of an imminent departure influenced it. Or did the Guggenheims give in to the owner's or the Housing Office's intense pressure? The following events lead to the latter assumption, for a few days later Salomon reported to the Housing Office that, despite considerable effort on his part, he had not been able to find a

---

[54] *Ibid.*, Memorandum of the Konstanz Housing Office, August 1, 1939.

Jewish landlord. He was therefore asking assignment to a place that had become available on Zogelmannstraße 16, one that belonged to the Jewish woman Berta Geismar. The request was then met with an order by the city on August 14, 1939: On September 1, the four Guggenheims moved into a 3-room apartment on Zogelmannstraße 16, only 100 meters from their old place on Hüetlinstraße.

Konstanz, den 17. November 1939.

Gesetz über Mietverhältnisse mit Juden,
- h i e r -

Beschluss:

Anwesen Zogelmannstrasse Nr. 16 in Konstanz.

I. An Herrn Salomon Israel Guggenheim, Konstanz, Schottenstrasse 75, an Frau Bona Sara Guggenheim, Konstanz, Schottenstrasse Nr. 75.-:

Ich ordne hiermit an, dass Sie die im Haus Zogelmann- strasse Nr. 16 in Konstanz durch den Wegzug der Familie Levinger frei gewordene Wohnung sofort zu beziehen haben.

II. Nachricht von Ziffer I dem Hausverwalter, Herrn Friedrich Mar- quardt, Jmmobilien, Konstanz, Bahnhofplatz Nr. 4.-

III. Zu den Akten:" Zogelmann- strasse Nr. 16. "

OB:

Jm Auftrag:

Direktor

M/Sdt.

gft.17.11.1939.

City of Konstanz order for the Guggenheim family to move to Zogelmannstraße 16
(Photo source: Konstanz City Archives)

Translation of the above:
Konstanz, November 17, 1939
Law Pertaining to Leases with Jews
<u>*Resolution:*</u>   *Property Zogelmannstrasse 16 in Konstanz*
I.   To Mr. Salomon Israel Guggenheim, Konstanz, Schottenstrasse 75,
To Mrs. Bona Sara Guggenheim, Konstanz, Schottenstrasse 75.
I hereby order you to move immediately into the apartment in the
building on Zogelmannstrasse 16, recently vacated by the Levinger family.
II. Report of Letter 1 of the building manager Mr. Friedrich Marquardt, Real
Estate,
Konstanz, Bahnhofplatz 4
III. For the files: "Zogelmannstrasse 16
Authorized by Director's Signature, November 17, 1939

After that, the orders regarding the move came thick and fast. Already on September 11, 1939, the city ordered the dissolution of the Guggenheim communal apartment: Bona and Dagobert would be "redirected" as subtenants of Leopold Rosenthal. The move took place on September 18, 1939. Salomon and Dagobert then registered a joint request with the Housing Office that both families be accommodated together for cost considerations, which the office director agreed to. Toni and Salomon again packed up their household belongings and moved to Schottenstraße as subtenants of the Julius Merzbacher family. But this was not to be their last move either: After the Levinger family vacated the Zogelmannstraße 16 residence, the city ordered the immediate removal of all four Guggenheims from the Schottenstraße to the Zogelmannstraße on November 17, 1939. This would remain their last address for just under a year until their deportation in October 1940. Bona, however, had only a few days with them to settle in. As mentioned, she was finally able to leave Germany at the beginning of December.

The Rosenwalds in Cologne were also affected by the concentration of Jewish citizens living in the rental properties. In February 1940, they received notification that they had to leave their residence at Antwerpener Straße 32 and move into a place in the Lindenburger Allee 26 in the Lindenthal district as of March 1.[55]

Condemned to Waiting and Hoping

We learn about the state of the Guggenheims' emigration attempts in Konstanz and of Lisel's in Cologne, as well as the developments of the relationship between Lisel and Dagobert from the details of the Rosenwalds' many letters.

It's also clear that Fritz, who has "americanized" his first name and now calls himself Fred, has taken a lot of time replying to the many letters from Cologne, as well as complying with the paperwork for the immigration of his sister Lisel – all of this, in addition to the costs he had to pay from his meager salary in the beginning. These heavy demands may have been a reason for neglecting his contact with Isi Guggenheim in Buenos Aires at that time. Isi complained about this in several of his letters to the Rosenwalds in Cologne.[56]

---

[55] Correspondence … 1940, letter Lisel R. of February 8, 1940, item 18.
[56] Correspondence … 1939, letter Lisel and Johanna R. of May 4, 1939, item 59.

It may be assumed that Isi, too, frequently wrote to his parents in Konstanz, but unfortunately, those letters no longer exist, all cards and letters addressed to his parents being lost after their deaths. And any letters Isi received in Argentina from his parents were not saved either. With that, the details of Isi's efforts on behalf of his parents' immigration to Argentina are unknown.

For all of 1939 and almost all of 1940, Salomon, Toni and Dagobert Guggenheim sat on their packed suitcases in Konstanz waiting for a visa for immigration to Argentina, or even to Chile as a transit country. Especially Dagobert went through a roller coaster of emotions. He had said his good-bye to Lisel several times, ever in anticipation of an imminent departure. But time and again, delays arose due to new regulations.

In August 1939, Dagobert, who went to the Argentine Consulate in Hamburg, learns that the disbursed travel costs no longer suffice. At least half of the total amount for the four Guggenheims should have been paid in foreign currency, and as of October, all costs have to be paid that way.[57] When Bona then was to emigrate by herself according to the decision of the family, Dagobert, who was very close with his mother, went into a serious depression. Lisel describes him as desperate, "losing his mind" and she tries to cheer him up.[58]

All in all, this practical young woman seems much more relaxed during this time, which is also critical for her. She reacts with gallows humor to the delays in the letter to her brother: *"We're still sitting in the holding pattern " (German: "Wir sitzen noch immer auf der Wartburg").*[59]

She is not doing any better in Cologne, after all; the immigration authorities in the USA are delaying the issuance of entry visas, probably also as a result of Germany's act of war on September 1, 1939. One time her brother's affidavit became invalid, as too much time had elapsed between its being issuance and the audit date. Then the new affidavit is deemed insufficiently qualified, because it is questionable whether the guarantor (Fritz) can offer enough long-term security.[60]

From the description of the most recent events, it is clear that Lisel's and Dagobert's relationship has become more serious. They are in constant communication about their efforts to gain an entry visa and they share their disappointment about the runaround they get from the authorities in charge.

---

[57] Correspondence ... 1939, letter Lisel R. of August 10, 1939, item 117.
[58] Correspondence ... 1940, letter Lisel R. of August 23, 1939, item 121.
[59] Correspondence ... 1940, letter Lisel R. of March 3, 1940, item 27.
[60] Correspondence ... 1939, letter Lisel R. of November 29, 1939, item 154; of January 5, 1940, item 3.

To be better supports for each other, they now plan to emigrate together. Although they are not thinking about marriage, they are considering going to England as a domestics couple.[61] England becomes the focus, because Lisel had already applied there for emigration quite a while ago, even before she tried to get to the USA.

This development makes clear that both of them were caught in a frantic rush, perhaps even desperation, and were now grasping at every straw. But the prospects for England were even more dismal, because, for one thing, the admission capacity was substantially smaller than for the USA, and for another, the required affidavits could not be obtained from the relatives living there.

In the course of 1940, when the war had spread to large areas of Europe and an ever increasing number of Jewish refugees in the German-occupied countries was pushing to go abroad, the USA and the South American countries tightened their immigration requirements more and more. The applications were now selected by the monetary amount in the affidavit. Then health and language tests were introduced. In addition, affidavits from a war-neutral third country were no longer accepted. This is what happened to Dago's friend from Konstanz, Hans Picard, who was later his companion into misfortune, for whom a relative in Switzerland provided an affidavit for entry to the USA in vain.[62]

Lisel and Dago looked for other places of refuge as well; Dago registered for emigration to the USA at the end of May, but had to expect a long wait with the Registration No. 54,936.[63] A few months later, they think about whether Dago should apply in Berlin for emigration to Santo Domingo.[64]

A brief window opened for Lisel's emigration to the USA in June 1940 on a somewhat adventurous route via Mandchuko and Yokohama. The emigration failed, however, because brother Fritz could not get a ship reservation in time.[65]

In September, Dago's and Lisel's relationship takes a remarkable turn – a partnership of convenience blossoms into a romantic attachment. Lisel, who had been doing piecework in a dressmaking factory the entire time, travels to Lake Konstanz for convalescent vacation. She is able to live with the Guggenheims in Konstanz. She is heartily welcomed in the

---

[61] Correspondence … 1939, letter Lisel R. of June 7, 1939, item 81.
[62] Correspondence … 1940, letter Lisel R. of August 17, 1940, item 95.
[63] Correspondence … 1940, letter Lisel R. of June 9, 1940, item 66.
[64] Correspondence … 1940, letter Lisel R. of August 30, 1940, item 100.
[65] Correspondence … 1940, letter Lisel R. of June 27, 1940, item 75.

Zogelmannstraße by Isi's mother Toni and accompanied by the two men, Salomon and Dagobert.

Dagobert introduces Lisel to his Konstanz circle of friends. Lisel gets to know all the men in the group photo on page ... The picture must have been taken in the fall. At the latest during this visit, about which she enthusiastically writes to brother, Lisel is very much in love with Dago. She has decided to marry him and to emigrate with him, either to the USA or even to Argentina. She weighs the option of Argentina in consideration of Dago, because she knows that he continues to have a strong connection to his mother in Buenos Aires.

Remarkably resolute, Lisel immediately goes about implementing her decision – still in Konstanz, she informs her brother, as well as Dago's mother about her decision to marry Dago and asks both for their approval. She also asks her brother for understanding that with this decision all the plans, as well as the efforts and costs of the entry to the USA to this date are now void.[66] She can take for granted her parents' approval in Cologne. Johanna and Karl Rosenwald, who know Dago well from his visits to Cologne, agree to the long-term connection between Lisel and Dago anyway.

Dago, doing forced labor in the Konstanz brickyard, cannot be with Lisel as much as he would like, but Lisel enjoys her vacation in the beautiful surroundings. She takes trips to places on the other side of lake, as for instance, Meersburg. Dago still has some money received by the Guggenheims from the sale of their property. With that, he can give Lisel gifts like a wristwatch.[67]

Toni, Dago and Salomon use this opportunity to add their greetings to the letter Lisel writes from Konstanz to her brother Fritz on September 15 (see p. ...). They confirm that they, too, are enjoying the time with Lisel and inform their friend in the USA, that Isi has "taken root" in Argentina. And yet, a certain resignation is palpable from the notes of the three Guggenheims; they are disappointed about their failed emigration attempts and currently see no chance of getting out of Germany.

---

[66] Correspondence ... 1940, letters Lisel R. of September 15, 1940, item 102, of September 26, 1940, item 106.
[67] ebenda

A group letter from top to bottom: Toni, Dagobert and Salomon Guggenheim to Fritz Rosenwald in New York, September 1940 (Photo source: Joan Fradkin)

Lisel would gladly have remained with Dago in Konstanz, but she was unable to find a job there. After she had already overstayed her vacation time, she returned to her parents in Cologne on September 24.[68]

What none of them could know was that the farewell from Dago, as well as from Isi's parents, Toni and Salomon, was to be a final farewell for Lisel. They would never see each other again. Less than four weeks later, the Guggenheims were forced to leave Konstanz and Germany forever. In contrast, Lisel and her parents in Cologne still had a "reprieve" of over a year, before they, too, were forcibly deported on December 1941 – the final destination being Riga in Latvia.[69]

Deportation to France on October 22, 1940

Meanwhile, the three remaining Guggenheims had continued to hope for an entry permit to one of the South American countries. When the Chilean government again put into force a strict exclusion policy against Jewish refugees as of 1940,[70] Salomon turned his eyes toward Argentina and asked his son Isi to try there to arrange for the immigration of his parents. In contrast, Dagobert continued to plan for his departure to Chile, as documents about his later internment in France show.[71]

The Guggenheims remained in the waiting position well into 1940. In the meantime, the German *Wehrmacht* [Army] had completed its triumphal march through western Europe with a victory over France and had divided the country into two zones of control. After the armistice of June 1940, the northern part of France was directly controlled by the German *Wehrmacht*. The southern part remained unoccupied for the time being. The French Vichy government, which was dependent on the German regime, exercised administrative sovereignty here. The German successes had increased the

---

[68] ebenda

[69] The details of the Cologne transport of December 7, 1941 to Riga can be found in Wolfgang Scheffler and Diana Schulle, *"Buch der Erinnerung. Die ins Baltikum deportierten deutschen, österreichischen und tschechoslovakischen Juden"* Bd.2 [The German, Austrian and Czechoslovakian Jews deported to the Baltic States, vol. 2], K.G. Saur, München 2003.

[70] As of 1940, only 88 Jews who lived in Baden-Württemberg as of 1933 found refuge in Chile. (Saur, op.cit., p. 240).

[71] In a written statement of "Camp de Gurs" on March 8, 1941, advocating for Dagobert's transfer to the *Les Milles* transit camp, it is noted that Dagobert was registered since November 19, 1939 with the Chilean Consulate in Bremen with Application No. 2140. Source: Archives Départementales (AD) Basses-Pyrénées, Pau.

support for the Nazi regime to such an extent in the greater population in Germany that the repressive measures against the Jews aroused less and less dissent.

It may also have been the minimal dismay shown by a large portion of the population toward the actions against their Jewish fellow citizens that removed any remaining scruples on the part of the Nazi rulers when, in a lightning operation on October 22 and 23, they deported 6,500 Jews from the southwestern districts Baden and Saarpfalz to Camp de Gurs in France at the foot of the Pyrenees. And the Nazi party's and regime's calculation about the population's reaction was in keeping with reality. Upon the completed deportation, Reinhard Heydrich, the head of the security police (SIPO) and the security services (SD) laconically informed the Department of State on October 29: *"The process of the operation was scarcely noticed by the residents."[72]* The eager and ambitious *Gauleiter* [district leaders] Robert Wagner (Baden) and Josef Bürckel (Saarpfalz) wanted to be the first to report their districts to the "Führer" Adolf Hitler as *judenrein* [free of Jews]. It is to their "credit" that with their sweeping human abduction operation, they opened the door to the Holocaust.

How the news of the imminent deportation reached the Guggenheims and what reactions it aroused in the residents of Zogelmannstraße has not been noted for posterity. A few survivors later recounted the process of the Konstanz deportation.[73]

On October 22, 1940, the last day of *Sukkot,* (the Feast of the Tabernacles), the usually happy Jewish festival, the Gestapo appeared early in the morning at the buildings inhabited by Jews and ordered the residents to be ready for departure within 30 to 60 minutes. They would be allowed to take 50 kilos of belongings, two days' worth of food and 100 RM per person. Shortly thereafter, those rounded up were transported in cars to the Petershausen freight train station and consigned to a passenger train with antiquated cars.

A total of 108 Jewish residents, including the three Guggenheims as the last remaining inhabitants of the house on Zogelmannstrafe 16 and two

---

[72] Stuttgart Archives management (ed.) *Dokumente über die Verfolgung der jüdischen Bürger im Baden-Württemberg durch das Nationalsozialistische Regime 1933-1945, Band 2* [The Persecution of the Jewish Citizens of Baden-Württemberg by the Nazi Regime 1933-1945, Volume 2]. (Stuttgart: 1966), p. 2.

[73] Erhard Roy Wiehn, *Oktoberdeportation 1940* (Konstanz, 1990); including Trudy Rothschild, *Die Verfolgung der badischen und pfälzischen Juden* [The Persecution of the Baden and Palatinate Jews], p. 167ff; Hugo Schriesheimer, *Die Hölle von Gurs* [The Hell of Gurs], p. 181ff.

visitors, were deported. The swift round-up of the Jewish residents was made very convenient by their concentration in the Jewish houses that had already been organized the previous year.

Although the so-called "Bürckel Operation" happened like a raid, just like the successful strategy of the *Blitzkriege* [lightning wars] and *Blitzfeldzüge* [lightning campaigns], they were planned well in advance, though not discernible to those affected by them. It is only in boarding the train that previously perceived abnormalities made sense to Hugo Schriesheimer:

"When I happened to go from the Marktstätte *[market place] across the railway tracks to the harbor, I saw a long train standing on the siding.... I couldn't figure out why it was there. A few days later I knew. It was the deportation train for the Jews...."*[74]

With each groups' departure from their residences, the SS security guards took the building keys and sealed off the apartments. All the furnishings, as well as all the valuables and belongings, were left and later were only rarely reclaimed by the survivors or their relatives. This also included the household items that Salomon Guggenheim had already listed two years before for the planned departure to Argentina.

The legal protection of this cold-blooded expropriation followed a year later: With the *11th Regulation of the Reich's Citizen Laws of November 25, 1941,* many of the Jews living abroad were declared *stateless.* From this retraction of citizenship, the German Reich logically derived the right to acquire the entire property, assets, and other claims of the emigrants. The assets were reprivatized at public auctions – this time changed to "Aryan" ownership – at prices generally far below market value.

In Konstanz, the auctions took place at the Council Building. Which buyers obtained the Guggenheims' abandoned furniture, household goods, silverware and valuable jewelry was not researched in the course of Isi Guggenheim's 1957 reparation court case, in which he invested much time and effort.

Just as the deportations of the other two districts did not arouse protest among the population, so it was in Konstanz.[75] Even the neighbors watched in silence. As would come to light later, this criminal operation – a clear violation of human rights – continued to be largely unnoticed even into the

---

[74] Schriesheimer, *op. cit.,* p. 183.
[75] *Ibid.*

present.[76] And yet it was a spectacular, one-of-a-kind operation. The October deportation signified the end of the already constrained Jewish life in Baden and Saarpfalz.

Thus, the *Kehilla Kedoscha Konstanz,* the Jewish Federation of Konstanz, founded in 1867, also ceased to exist.

Deportation of the Jews of Gailingen, October 22, 1940 (Photo source: E. Friedrich/D. Schmieder)

Camp Gurs as a Transit Station into the Unknown

The Konstanz Jews had to wait a while for the departure from the Petershausen station in the train prepared for them. In the late afternoon on October 22, 1940, around 6 p.m., the train began to roll. In Singen, a larger group joined them: They were the Jews of the Hegau villages of Gailingen and Randegg. Among them were two of Salomon's siblings: older sister

---

[76] Hans-Hermann Seiffert, *Entrechtet – verschleppt – ermordet, Der Weg der Konstanzer Jüdin Johanna Hammel in die Gaskammer von Auschwitz-Birkenau* [Disenfranchised – Deported – Murdered, the Journey of the Konstanz Jewish Woman Johanna Hammel to the Gas Chamber of Auschwitz-Birkenau]. (Konstanz, 2007), pp. 7-8.

Adele, now a Rothschild, and younger brother Siegfried Guggenheim, both of Randegg. It may be assumed that the siblings met there or at least saw each other there. Less likely, however, is that they traveled together from then on. The departing groups, assembled in each community, were under strict supervision by the escorting security teams and could not change train cars at the stations.

Gradually the compartments filled up with people of various ages[77] at the next stations in Donaueschingen, Villingen and Offenburg. The route went via Kehl-Straßburg through the German-occupied part of France. Chalon-sur-Saône was a border-crossing to the unoccupied southern zone. Lyon and Toulouse were next en route before the train pulled into Oloron-Sainte-Marie, the closest station to Gurs, on October 24, 1940. After a last overnight stay in the train, the deportees were transported the next morning on October 25, 1940 on open trucks to Camp Gurs at the foot of the Pyrenees.

Dago had evidently succeeded – either from Konstanz or on the way – in informing Lisel of the deportation of the Konstanz Jews. On October 26, shortly after the deportees had arrived in Camp de Gurs, she shared with her brother:

"Dago went somewhere with Isi's parents. I don't know anything about him and surely, he is alright... It's a good thing I was at Dago's during my vacation, as all of his friends and acquaintances are traveling."[78]

Lisel uses the term "traveling" for the forced deportation. It is one of the euphemistic concepts during this time of persecution that was frequently used by the deportees when they sent messages out of the camps to their relatives or friends. They knew their cards and letters would be censored, so they had to transmit the bad news in code. In addition, since the beginning of the war in September 1939, mail going to other countries was censored by the German OKW[79], as shown by the envelopes in Cologne of Fritz Rosenwald's estate. In the files of the communities carrying out the deportations there are also euphemistic expressions for the expulsion of Jewish citizens.[80]

---

[77] The ages of the deported Konstanz Jews ranged from 92 (Charlotte Bloch) to 3 years (Ruth Alexander). See Bloch, *op. cit.*, pp. 271-272.
[78] Correspondence ... 1940, letter Lisel R. of October 26, 1940, item 127.
[79] OKW = **O**ber**K**ommando der **W**ehrmacht (Senior Command of the Army)
[80] In the Konstanz residents registry, deportations are called "evacuations".

Camp de Gurs was a large internment complex, having already been built in April 1939 to take in the refugees of the Spanish Civil War. Later, after the outbreak of World War II, refugees, who emigrated in the 1930s from Germany to France, were also interned here.[81] In May 1940, after the German *Wehrmacht*'s occupation of the Netherlands and Belgium, Jews from those countries were also sent there.

Camp de Gurs, at right the long camp road, ca. 1939 (Photo source: Claude Laharie, *Gurs: 1939-1945*)

The camp was divided into 13 alphabetically marked sections, so-called *ilôts* [islets] with 25 barracks each. Crammed into each barracks were 50 to 60 people. Women and men were segregated into separate *ilôts*. The adminstration was the responsibility of the civil offices of the Vichy regime, and security detail was provided by the French gendarmes.

Gurs was not a concentration camp in the German sense. And perhaps a bit of comfort for the terrible shock experienced by the Jews of Baden and Saarpfalz upon their arrival may have been the fact of no longer having to live in the immediate control area of the Nazi rulers. Completely wet from a

---

[81] Among the most well-known prisoners were the philosopher Hannah Arendt, the author Jean Améry, the actress Dita Parlo and the Social Democrat parliamentarian Hedwig Kämpfer. See Edwin M. Landau, Samuel Schmitt *Lager in Frankreich* [Camps in France] (Mannheim: 1991), p. 28.

soaking rain, they were assigned to their quarters that offered them only a place with a straw bags. There were no furnishings, no beds, no food nor acceptable latrines. Hanna Schramm, a non-Jewish immigrant from Berlin, gives an impressive description of the situation and the horror:

"The service barracks were full of women staring at us with incredible fatigue, numb apathy, flickering fear and were close to fainting. There came... more old ones ... figures from the grave, helpless and no longer of this world. "[82]

To breathe a bit of courage into these unfortunate people and give them a bit of orientation, Berthold Wieler, the head of the former Konstanz Jewish Community, accommodated almost all the Konstanzers in one barracks. Thus, the majority of the men – among them Salomon and Dagobert Guggenheim – were housed in Ilôt E, Barracks 16. The Konstanz women,, including Toni Guggenheim, were mostly in Ilôt K in Barracks 12 and 13.

After the instructions by the French command, the new "residents" began to organize their lives as well as they could. In every *ilôt*, a field kitchen was established, the leaking roofs and walls were temporarily repaired and heating material for the stoves was found. Salomon and other occupants of the men's Barracks E 16 sent a note for help to the Jewish Federation in Kreuzlingen, Switzerland, Konstanz's neighboring city. They asked for packages of food, warm clothing, medicine, as well as money, so they could buy the most necessary items from the canteen run by Spanish mercenaries.[83]

---

[82] Barbara Vormeier, *Die Deportierungen deutscher und österreichischer Juden aus Frankreich* [The Deportations of German and Austrian Jews from France] (Paris: 1980), p. 16.
[83] Letter of November 1, 1940, in: Wiehn, *Oktoberdeportation 1940*, p. 620.

Central soup kitchen in an *ilôt* in Gurs, 1941 (Photo source: Claude Laharie, *Gurs: 1939-1945*)

But for the time being the living conditions continued to be catastrophic, as the food was of poor quality and inadequate quantity. The indisputably poor hygienic conditions with few latrines that were hard to access, as well as rats and fleas in the barracks, led to an outbreak of influenza and diarrhea of life-threatening severity. In the first winter of 1940-41, hundreds of the Jews interned in Gurs died. Among them were Salomon's two Randegg siblings: The registered dates of death for Adele Rothschild is November 18, 1940, and December 8, 1940 for Siegfried Guggenheim.[84] Both are buried in the large cemetery in Gurs.

---

[84] Baden-Württemberg State Archive Directorate (ed.). *Die Opfer der nationalsozialistischen Judenverfolgung in Baden-Württemberg 1933-1945* [The Victims of the Nazi Persecution of Jews in Baden-Württemberg 1933-1945] (Stuttgart: 1969), pp. 105; 294.

Truck with coffins in Camp Gurs (Photo source: Guttermann/Morgenstern, *The Gurs Haggadah*)

Grave of Siegfried Guggenheim, Camp Gurs Cemetery (Photo credit: H.-H. Seiffert)

Gradually the provisions improved for those internees who were supported with packages from obliging relatives and friends in the neutral countries. Konstanz Jews received food and clothing from the Jewish Community in neighboring Kreuzlingen and with that agency passing on the word to the Swiss Federation of Jewish Communities in St. Gallen. This Jewish community also tried to find out whether there could be a release from the camp and researched the emigration possibilities. The latter effort was especially important for those who had already submitted applications and could show affidavits, guarantees from the host country and registration numbers.

Because of this, the three Guggenheims, having already submitted emigration applications in Konstanz to Argentina and Chile, hoped soon to leave the inhumane conditions of this internment. What they probably did not see as an acceptable option – given the present political situation – is returning to their homeland. The other option, the worst of all outcomes, was not even thinkable at that point.

The travel routes from France to overseas countries, which were still open in 1940, were not available to the Guggenheims, as the French Ministry of the Interior was only rarely issuing emigration visas to German emigrants after the cease-fire. The French regime justified this by stating that it had to wait for the extradition lists of the Armistice Commission.[85]

Seemingly Closer to the Safe Haven in Les Milles

In the spring of 1941, the Guggenheims had reason for new hope. They were transferred from Camp Gurs to Camp Les Milles, a suburb of Aix-en-Provence. At that time, it had the status of a transit camp. Because of its proximity to the Marseille harbor, those refugees who had applied for emigration overseas and to neutral European countries were collected there.

The transfer for all three did not, however, occur on the same day. Salomon and Toni were the first to leave Gurs on February 28, 1941, after the camp administration had approved the transfer to Les Milles with an *avis favorable* [favorable opinion]. The basis of the decision was the confirmation of the emigration applications being processed by the Argentine Consulate in Marseille, the couple having access to 10,000 French

---

[85] The Commission under the leadership of Legation Counselor Ernst Kundt was to produce a list of names of those refugees in southern France who were valid "Aryans" and could be repatriated.

francs in cash and having payment for the travel costs guaranteed by relatives in Argentina.[86]

Registration of arrival and departure of Salomon and Toni Guggenheim in the Les Milles transit camp, Salomon's camp number at left (Photo source: Archives Départementales Basses Pyrénées (AD) Marseille)

---

[86] Notes of the *Commissaire spécial chef de service* in Gurs, February 1941 (no day of the month given) to the prefects in Pau (Basses Pyrénées). Source: Archives Départementales Basses Pyrénées, Pau.

Dagobert followed two weeks later on March 16, 1941. His transfer hinged on instructions to check with the Chilean Consulate in Marseille about the transit visa he had applied for. He was given the camp number 1,153. His application for the transfer to Marseille included the notation that he had access to 3,000 French francs and that his brother-in-law Ludovico (Ludwig) Strauss in Buenos Aires would pay for the travel costs.

As in Gurs, the women and children were housed separately from the men, but this time with a greater distance between them. The Les Milles camp had set up a branch location in Marseille. It consisted of quarters in three hotels in different areas, the "Bompard," "Terminus des Ports" and "Levant." Toni, who had a *sauf-conduit* [safe conduct], a permit issued in Pau, was registered at the "Terminus des Ports" on the Boulevard des Dames immediately upon arrival in Marseille. There she was given a *récépissé* [receipt], a certificate with a passport photo stating that she had applied for a passport. She was given a temporary right of residence until August 30, 1941.

Hotel "Terminus des Ports," Marseille, 1941 (Photo source: Musée Mémorial de la Shoah, Paris)

Salomon and Dagobert, on the other hand, had to stay in Camp Les Milles about 30 kilometers away.

What were the living conditions like in Camp Les Milles? The camp was situated in a brickyard and factory at the west exit of the village of Les Milles. The impressive-looking building was three stories tall, but because of economic problems, the factory had been closed since 1938. At the beginning of the war in early September 1939, the military authorities took over the building and housed soldiers there. Later in the spring and summer of 1940, emigrants living in France were already interned there. Some well-known names were among them: the authors Lion Feuchtwanger, Alfred Kantorowicz, the artists Max Ernst and Max Lingner, the historian Golo Mann. They came into the country to save themselves mostly through illegal channels.

It was not only the fact of being closer to the Marseille, the port of departure, that the Guggenheims felt they were better off at the current internment site. They also appreciated the accommodations, which offered better protection from the weather, as well as the chance for the couples to meet outside of a fenced-in camp.

A month after arriving in Marseille, Toni Guggenheim shared her satisfaction in a letter to Erna Veit[87] in Kreuzlingen, Switzerland:

" ...we went through some hard times in Gurs, but are now hopeful that we will be able to endure further difficulties and reach our goal in good health. "[88]

Until November 1940, Camp Les Milles functioned as an internment camp. Thereafter, it was converted to a transit camp for taking in foreigners awaiting departure. The Interior Ministry of the Vichy regime, having taken over the administration of the camp from the Ministry of War, ordered comprehensive structural changes to the facility so the emigrants could have "normal" living conditions. The security personnel were switched from soldiers to police.

---

[87] Erna Veit was the sister of Johanna Hammel and daughter of Lina Hammel, who was housed in the same barracks in Gurs with Toni Guggenheim.

[88] Letter of April 17, 1941, in: E.R. Wiehn, *Die bittere Not begreifen. Deutsch-jüdische Deportiertenpost aus südfranzösischen Interniergungslagern [Understanding the Bitter Need. German-Jewish Deportees' Mail from Southern France Internment Camps]*, Hartung-Gorre Verlag, Konstanz 2016, p. 83.

Les Milles brickyard (Photo source: Mémorial du Camp des Milles)

Village of Les Milles, postcard from the 1930s (Photo source: D. Obschernitzki, *Letzte Hoffnung – Ausreise* [Last Hope – Emigration])

As of the middle of December 1940, the camp filled up with emigrants and deportees who applied for departure. The structural changes had increased the housing capacity to 1,300 beds in the three stories of the brick factory, and while the building did offer better weather protection than Camp Gurs, the poor nutrition and inadequate sanitary conditions made the stay there anything but pleasant. To escape this misery even for a short time, the internees frequently took advantage of the camp's exit provision: They were given a temporary leave pass for visits to agencies regarding their planned departure and to hospitals in Aix-en-Provence and Marseille. In Marseille, the men could then get together with the women in the three hotels.

Internees in the open space of the Les Milles brickyard (Photo source: Grandjonc/Grundtner, *Zone der Ungewissheit* [Zone of Uncertainty])

In March 1941, at the same time of the Guggenheims' arrival in Les Milles, the HICEM,[89] a Jewish aid organization, opened an office in the camp. It received a list of the new arrivals from the camp administration. HICEM was to play an important role in securing the flight of many emigrants, especially in the later "Final Solution" phase, when legal departure was no longer possible from France. The organization's mission was finding berths on ships, and it often made monies available for the payment of such passages.

---

[89] HICEM is combination of **Hi**as, **JCA** and **EMIGDIRECT**, all three being Jewish emigration organizations.

It was not possible to determine whether the Guggenheims had contact with HICEM about receiving support for their emigration efforts. If they did, this aid organization was not able to save them, as the course of events will show.

Long Months Between Hope and Fear in Les Milles

We know that the emigration efforts of the three Guggenheims had been underway since the beginning of 1939 with the help of their relatives in Argentina. As already mentioned, the French government, with few exceptions, stopped issuing emigration visas in the latter half of 1940. That made a legal exit almost impossible.

We know from the oral descriptions of the Argentine descendants of the deported Guggenheims, however, that during 1941 and 1942 Isi Guggenheim and the Strauss relatives in Buenos Aires did everything they could by contacting the Argentine and Chilean Consulates in Marseille to obtain departure permits for their relatives interned in Les Milles.

To gauge the obstacles of the would-be emigrees and their supporters abroad in procuring the longed-for travel ticket, a short description of the bureaucratic hurdles to be overcome is in order here. First, it was not easy to get a berth on a ship with a limited number available. Apart from that, the South American Marseille-Buenos Aires shipping line was discontinued as of January 1941, shortly after the liner *Mendoza* was captured by a British warship.[90] When the next best carrier to South America, the Antillen shipping line, canceled its passages too, the ship traffic from Marseille was restricted to connections with the North African Mediterranean harbors of Oran and Casablanca. From there, the internees had to find a way across the ocean.

In addition, all the various necessary applications and forms had to be validated simultaneously and coordinated at the right time. Although the Vichy government had loosened its emigration visa restrictions in January 1941, granting such visas by the transit countries and the tighter entry conditions of the host countries still presented problems.

---

[90] Doris Obschernitzki, *Letzte Hoffnung – Ausreise, Die Ziegelei von Les Milles* [Last Hope – Emigration, The Brickyard of Les Milles] (Aix-en-Provence, 1939-42 Hentrich & Hentrich, Teetz, 1999), p. 200.

Marseille harbor, location of hope for so many refugees
(Quelle: Doris Obschernitzki "Letzte Hoffnung – Ausreise")

The entry permit to Argentina, the *llamada,* was already hard to get for Jewish refugees in 1941 under the Castillo government, which sympathized with the Nazi rulers. Even when the Jewish refugees were able to get the *llamada,* however, the missing passport from their native country was enough for the Argentine Consulates to deny the issuance of an immigration visa.[91]

And this was the obstacle the Guggenheims could not get around. Their passports had been taken away from them at the time of deportation in Konstanz, and they had been unable to obtain new valid passports in France. Thus, a legal exit was barred for them.

The Guggenheims in Les Milles were well aware of this bitter consequence.

---

[91] The Jewish man, Semi Uffenheimer of Baden, who was staying in French Free Zone outside of Camp de Gurs in August 1941, reported on these experiences, source: Gabriel Groszman, *Semi Uffenheimer, jüdische Familiengeschichten aus Breisach, Lörrach, Bühl, Graben in Baden und in Argentinien, [Jewish Family Stories from Breisach, Lörrach, Bühl, Graben in Baden and in Argentina]*, Hartung-Gorre Verlag, Konstanz 2013, p. 196; similarly a shared experience in *Aides Aux Émigrés, Section Suisse Genf* of February 5, 1942.

A few letters exist in which they express their hopeless situation. Those show their efforts, the failures and the mood of the three interned family members in Les Milles camp and in Hotel "Terminus" in Marseille. All endeavors undertaken by Isi, as well as the Strauss family in Buenos Aires, had fallen through.

Salomon's letter of July 1, 1941, to Erna Veit at the office of the Jewish Community in Kreuzlingen is suffused with a deep sense of resignation.

He thanks Erna for a financial contribution that the former Konstanz resident gathered through donations for the deported Konstanzers with her unceasing commitment to them.[92] Then he deplores his and his relatives' futile situation in gaining entry to Argentina:

"Our wish to be with our dear Isi soon has, unfortunately, not been fulfilled, since we need our passports for the registration of the visas and the Konstanz passport office is not issuing them, despite complaints lodged from various sides, and our Isi has done everything that could possibly be done and has prepared everything for us."

The position of the Konstanz Passport Office is an example for clearly showing that even in a "normal" agency, like the city administration and finance authorities, the office was staffed by complicit bureaucrats who intentionally or unintentionally provided concrete assistance to the SS and Gestapo criminals, especially with the systematic murder of the European Jews.

Nor does Salomon harbor much hope for success with the Argentine emigration:

"May G.w. ["God be willing"–Ed.] *to find a way for us somehow to let us have our long-awaited wish."*

Most distressing for Salomon was his wife Toni's poor state of health with her heart ailment. A passport photo attached to the granting of a *récépissé* identity card in May 1941 clearly shows her to be marked by the hardships of the internment. It is also possible that the failed emigration efforts had affected the couple emotionally. At the same time, the letter does not express the desperation that would be evident if they thought themselves to be in a life-threatening situation. They were still outside of the Nazi rulers' direct

---

[92] The author wrote about the fate of the deported relatives of Erna Veit in Seiffert, *Johanna Hammel, op. cit.*

sphere of violence. And as long as that was the case, they could hope to leave Europe and reach a safe haven.

Months later, Dago again has to admit in a letter to Fritz Rosenwald that he no longer has any hope of emigrating to South America:

"Everything humanly possible has been tried and still we have not reached our goal. One obstacle after another has been put in our way... With us, the passport was missing and not obtainable... The current situation for our departure is completely negative, certainly to South America."[94]

But it is not only the fear of his own fate and that of his family that weighs on Dago at the this time – the end of November 1941. From Cologne, he learns from Lisel, with whom he continued to have close correspondence, that the Rosenwalds, too, now had to leave Germany. Their prospects are far more unfortunate than the Guggenheims'. Quite in contrast to the Jews of Baden the year before, the destination of the Cologne Jews transport is not Western Europe, but the East.

And even more depressing is that the deportations remain in their persecutors' direct area of influence. Since the German "Wehrmacht" (Army) opened a new front with its Russian campaign in June 1941, thereby occupying new lands in the East, the "Volksfeinde" (enemies of the people) – the Jews – could now be taken out of the Reich (homeland) and concentrated in camps in the occupied territories. The administration of these camps was securely in the hands of the German SS, the ruthless unit of the Nazi Party, to whom the decision-making powers for the fate of the European Jews had been assigned by the Reich government.[95]

---

[94] Letter by Dagobert G. of November 30, 1941 to Fritz R., op. cit., correspondence from others 1937-1941, items 10 and 11.

[95] In a letter of July 31, 1941, the Reich Minister Hermann Göring, had authorized Reinhard Heydrich, Head of the RSHA (Reichssicherheits-Hauptamt – Reich Main Security Office) to prepare "a complete solution for the Jewish Question in the German sphere of influence in Europe."

Salomon Guggenheim's letter to the supporters Kreuzlingen, Switzerland (Photo source: Yad Vashem Archives, Jerusalem). See appendix for typed and translated version.

But this state of quietude was deceptive. What the Guggenheims and other internees could not know is that the agencies of persecution in Berlin, as well as the Vichy regime's Interior Ministry, issued orders in the first half of 1941 that the emigration of the Jews interned in France should be prohibited *"in view of the certain upcoming 'final solution to the Jewish question.'"*[96]

Toni Guggenheim's application for an identification card, issued in Marseille, May 1941
(Photo source: AD Marseille)

---

[96] Letter by the RSHA of May 20, 1941, to the commissioners for the heads of the Security Police (SIPO) and the Security Services (SD) for Belgium and France, cited by Jacques Grandjonc, Theresia Grundtner."*Zone der Ungewißheit, Exil und Internierung in Südfrankreich 1933-1944* [Zone of Uncertainty, Exile and Internment in Southern France, 1933-1944] (Rowohlt, Reinbek, 1993), Appendix.

Jews from Baden in Les Milles waiting for departure (Photo source: Landau, Schmitt, *Lager in Frankreich* [Camps in France])

The Vichy government's anti-Jewish collaboration policies functioned, in effect, as an auxiliary to the Nazi regime, thereby shattering any chance of receiving a French emigration visa as of mid-1941. These policies undoubtedly stood in contradiction to the concept of the Les Milles transit camp. This led to the internees' camp detention being prolonged. With ever more Jews having applied for emigration visas and being transferred from Gurs to Les Milles as of the summer 1941, they now had to organize their lives in the camp.

The increasing food scarcity forced the inmates to buy basic food stuffs on the black market. Salomon, like the other men whose wives were interned in Marseille or who had business with the agencies, was able to make use of the generous temporary leave regulations of Camp Director Robert Maulavé. They organized schools and workshops, even a theatre troupe for entertainment.

A big problem, however, continued to be the ongoing lack of employment and resulting boredom. In June 1941, Vichy had imposed a stricter order forbidding all Jews from *"pursuing a profession that would bring them into contact with the public.*[100] In practice, this deprived them of any opportunity to earn a living.

At the same time, Dago did not want to be without work, so as of mid-November, he took on small projects in the camp:

"As of two weeks ago, I'm working as a laborer in the camp and hope to gain some benefits in time, the main one already being that I'm not brooding, but doing something useful and filling up my days."[101]

This regulation was relaxed in February and April 1942 when the Interior Ministry allowed the Les Milles camp director to employ the camp inmates in forestry work for a small compensation. The payroll for July and August 1942 shows Dagobert Guggenheim and another man from Konstanz, Simon Alexander, as workers. The pay amounted to barely 400 francs, or converted to 20 marks per month.[102]

For at least a year – from mid-1941 to August 1942 – the Guggenheims, with no inkling about the "final solution plans," waited for their hoped-for departures to Argentina and Chile. They shared the fate of roughly 1,300 Les Milles Jews interned and ready to emigrate, most of whom had also been deported from Baden and Saarpfalz. Only 274 of those held in Les Milles and the hotels of Marseille were able to cross the Mediterranean and emigrate to Oran or Casablanca from July 1941 to September 1942.[103] From there, they had to find an overseas ship. This travel was undertaken by illegal means without an emigration visa from the French authorities but almost always with the active organizational and financial support of HICEM or other emigration organizations.

The Missing Document for Freedom

The correspondence between Dago and Lisel kept going until the end of November 1941, until the time the Rosenwalds' were forced to deport with the third transport train collecting about 1,000 Jewish citizens in Cologne.

Up to that point, Dago and Lisel had each fought from their respective locations for emigration to their relatives living in safety. Lisel, who sees her

---

[100] Oberschernitzki, *op. cit.*, p. 243.

[101] Letter of Dago G. of November 30, 1941 to Fritz R., op.cit., correspondence from others ..., item 11..

[102] *"Borderaux des Sommes Versées aux Hébergés du Camp des Milles"* [Bordeaux amount paid to those hosted in Camp des Milles] Archives Départementales Des Bouches-du-Rhône, Marseille, File 142 W 29.

[103] Obschernitzki, *op. cit.*, p. 201.

future at Dago's side, considered her emigration to the New York only as a way station. The final destination is to be Buenos Aires or any other place where Dago would be safe.[104]

As the "rescuers" – Fritz in New York and Isi in Buenos Aires – did all they could to obtain the required affidavits, travel tickets, transit and entry visas. The costs for all of these documents and the extra expenses for telex approval by travel agents were covered by Fritz Rosenwald for Lisel, and by Bona Guggenheim for her relatives in Les Milles.

But always when one of the two – Lisel or Dago – had booked a passage on a ship and thought the departure was now a sure thing, something intervened – either the ship was overbooked or the host country passed a new regulation with restrictions affecting Lisel or Dago. Especially the events of the war had a negative effect on the immigration politics of the host countries. So, for instance, after the attack of Germany against the Soviet Union in June 1941, the American Consulate in Stuttgart closed its offices for several weeks, causing Lisel to continue to wait for her visa appointment. The U-boat war in the Atlantic led to delays, even cancellations of passages.

Lisel had even booked two passages: for July 28, 1941, with the "Nyassa" and for September 5 with the "Exeter" – both from Lisbon.[105] But she was still missing the visa from the American Consulate in Stuttgart. She learns from Dago that in Les Milles "everything is set for departure, except for the passports".[106] That is an essential missing paper that will not be provided in the future and which will become a "fata morgana" (mirage) for the Guggenheims in Buenos Aires.

At the beginning of June, the Rosenwalds receive the next blow: they have to move again within Cologne – back into the center of the city again to Bismarckstraße 10. The Cologne Gestapo had ordered that the " better" parts of the city were to be "judenrein" (free of Jews) as of June 1, 1941, and Lindenthal, in which the Rosenwalds resided, was one of those "better" areas.[107]

In their letters, Lisel and Johanna Rosenwald make clear that Fritz in New York is going all out in battling for the immigration of his sister. He has responded flexibly to all of Lisel's requests and change of plans. At the very

---

[104] Correspondence … 1940, Letter of Lisel to Fritz of October 26, 1940, item 128.
[105] Correspondence … 1941, Letter of Lisel to Fritz of May 25, 1941, item 49.
[106] Correspondence … 1941, Letter of Lisel to Fritz of April 29, 1941, item 38.
[107] *Die jüdischen Opfer des Nationalsozialismus aus Köln, Gedenkbuch [The Jewish Victims of the Nazi Era from Cologne, Memorial Book]*, Information from the State Archive of Cologne, Notebook 77, Cologne 1995, p. 534, footnote 24.

last, when the American Consulate in Stuttgart closed as of August 1941, Fritz tries to get the visa for Lisel through the Jewish aid organization HIAS (Hebrew Immigration Aid Society) and the central immigration office in Washington, DC. His efforts are in vain – families with children now have priority in the granting of a visa.

It is remarkable how Lisel and Dago try to support and encourage each other across the miles. Though they each must deal with their own disappointment, they still have the reserve to care about the partner and to do something for him or her. Lisel asks her brother to support Dago with non-perishable foodstuffs.[108] Dago gives Lisel the address of his cousin Marcel Guggenheim in Zurich, in case she needs his help, and he has money sent to her from his mother Bona. In addition – something that is vital during this time of unreliable postal service to and from Germany – the Zurich address is to be the contact address for Lisel and Dago's mail.[109]

Despite the intense exchange of information, Lisel does not have a clear picture of the Guggenheims' situation in Les Milles. Her hope that Dago, himself a prisoner in the camp, can find a way to get her out of Cologne and to him in Les Milles, is completely unrealistic.

But she has a more down-to-earth view of her own and her family's situation; she realizes that the imminent "evacuation" indicates a clear deterioration – perhaps even a life-threatening one – to the family's life circumstances. And in this perilous moment, she pleads with her brother once again "to pull out all the stops" and try every aid organization.[110] Finally, Lisel considers Cuba as the ultimate destination for herself and Dago. She has obtained information that no affidavit is necessary there for immigration. It would be possible to immigrate quickly, because the island nation needs young workers.[111] She urges Dago to convince his Argentine relatives to provide the hefty sum of $420 required for entry.

But now it becomes evident that these two partners have a different perspective of the seriousness of the situation. Lisel suspects that the deportation to the East will endanger her life, her mother's and especially that of her ailing father. Dago, on the other hand, in the Free Zone of France, is not directly under the thumb of German "Final Solution" enforcers; nor did he live through the acute threat to his life in Germany. He is, therefore,

---

[108] Correspondence … 1941, letter Lisel to Fritz of September 28, 1941, item 101.

[109] Dago describes his cousin Marcel Guggenheim as his "postillon d'amour" (go-between); correspondence from others, op. cit., item 10.

[110] Correspondence … 1941, letter of August 16, 1941, item 81.

[111] Correspondence … 1941, letter of Lisel to Fritz, September 9, 1941, item 95.

not yet ready to put aside his hesitations about asking his family for money.[112]

As soon became clear, even the availability of the requested money would not have helped. Dago and Lisel were not ready to fulfill a second important precondition for immigration – to submit a declaration of permanently settling in Cuba.

Shattered Hope for Emigration – Deportation to the East

During the last months of 1941, the situation becomes ever more precarious for Jews in Germany. Lisel is desperate about her food conditions. She writes her brother:

"...for someone somewhere has to help us, or we will perish wretchedly ...You can't imagine what it's like."[113]

There is a lot of unrest among the Jewish population of Cologne – the preparations for the first deportations of Jews to the East are beginning. All the Jewish resident are recorded by name and transport lists are created. In October, precisely on the 22nd and 30th, two transports with about 1,000 people leave Cologne for Litzmannstadt, the former Lodz, in Poland.

On October 26, 1941, Lisel reports to her brother that her family, too, has received notification for deportation, but that they are still deferred.[114] It may be assumed that the father's advanced age of 62[115] and his poor health were the cause of the delay. But Lisel sees clearly that her family has received only a reprieve and will surely be assigned to the next transport.

After the two deportations in short intervals, no other transport went from Cologne to Litzmannstadt. The hope arose that the transports to the East would be completely stopped. Dago, who continued to correspond with Lisel, received the news from her on November 13, that they still did not know whether or not her family could remain in Cologne.[116]

But it would not be long before a decision was made. In her last letter, dated November 29, Lisel informs her brother that they were preparing

---

[112] Correspondence ... 1941, letter of Lisel to Fritz, August 31, 1941, item 91.
[113] ebenda.
[114] Correspondence ....1941, letter of Lisel to Fritz, item 111.
[115] In her letter of November 8, 1941, Lisel mentions that people over 60 can be exempted from the deportations; correspondence ... 1941, item 114.
[116] Letter of Dago G. to Fritz R., November 30, 1941, op. cit., item 10.

themselves for the deportation. On November 13, the Gestapo orders the "Jüdische Kultusvereinigung Synagogengemeinde Köln" (Jewish Cultus Association Synagogue Community of Cologne) to inform all of the remaining 5,000 Jews of the city with a letter that they are to be ready for an imminent "evacuation". For the deportation, the euphemistic Nazi expression "evacuation" was used. All of the Cologne Jews received this letter. All had been informed, so everyone was affected.[117]

Because of the ailing father, the Rosenwalds made another request for deferral, but it was denied. The letter, however, did not state when and where the transport was to go, nor who would be on the transport list. But then, on November 29, as Lisel was sending her last letter to her brother, the notice of the Synagogue Community of Cologne had arrived at the Rosenwalds, informing them that they were to be at the collection point for the deportation – the Messe (convention hall) Cologne.

But still there is a slim hope that at least they will not be part of the next transport. There is a pre-selection, since the number of people exceeds the transport capacity of 1,000 people. The final determination of the travelers will be made at the collection point.[118]

It may be assumed that Lisel also informed Dago about this. But he will have received the news only in December 1941, about the time Fritz received it in New York.

In her last letter of November 29, 1941, mother and daughter thank Fritz for his never-ceasing efforts to bring Lisel to safety, and they assure him once again:

"You have really done in every way what you possibly could and have spent a lot of money."[119]

Lisel sends her luggage for storage to Marcel Guggenheim's address in Zurich. She also sends Fritz again the waiting number for the family's prospective emigration to the USA: Lisel's number is 12,770, her parents' is 27,945. They are still hoping to leave Germany.

---

[117] Dieter Corbach, *6.00 Uhr ab Messe Köln-Deutz Deportationen 1938-1945, [6 O'clock from the Messe Cologne-Deutz Deportations 1938-1945],* Scriba-Verlag, Köln 1999, p. 115.

[118] *Die jüdischen Opfer des Nationalsozialismus aus Köln, Gedenkbuch [The Jewish Victims of the Nazi Regime in Cologne, Memorial Book],* op. cit., p. 534.

[119] Correspondence ... 1941, letter of Lisel and Johanna, November 29, 1941, item 116.

In the Messe hall, the Rosenwalds' last hope of being excluded from the following day's deportation is shattered on December 6. They will not be removed from the list.

The third Cologne transport left the Deutz-Tief Station on December 7, 1941, with a new destination. The trip now went to Riga in Latvia. Originally, the destination was to be the White Russian city Minsk for a departure on December 8.

…Among the 1,011 Jewish people were Karl, Johanna and Lisel Rosenwald. For them, as for most of the deportees, this was to be a trip of no return.

Upon arrival in Riga on December 10, the deportees were sent to the ghetto "Moskauer Vorstadt" (Moscow Suburb), that had been opened up a few days before after a massacre of the Jewish Latvians.

With the deportation, the correspondence that Lisel had with her brother in New York, with Dago in Les Milles and occasionally with his mother in Bueno Aires stops. It can't be assumed that, from the collection point of the Cologne Messe, she was able to reach her relatives with a letter to inform them of the family's destination. In the ghetto, letters by the internees could neither be sent nor received.

Very little can be found about the continued fate of the three Rosenwalds in the Riga Ghetto. No clue has as yet been found about the parents Karl and Johanna. It is certain that they met their deaths in or outside the ghetto, either through sickness, debilitation or the frequent killing operations. [120]

---

[120] The author is basing his assumption on knowledge he gained from his research in Riga in combination with the fate of a Jewish family in his hometown: see *Hans-Hermann Seiffert, A Jewish Woman from Sehnde Comes Back, Gerda Rose Survives the Nazi Death Camps Jungfernhof, Kaiserwald and Stutthof as well as the Death March,* Hartung-Gorre Publishing, Konstanz/Germany 2018.

Karl and Johanna Rosenwald, Cologne, 1913; (Photo source: Joan Fradkin)

Murders of smaller numbers of victims often took place inside the ghetto, as well as later on the concentration camp grounds Kaiserwald. Mass shooting of larger numbers of ghetto residents were carried out outside of the ghetto in the woods of Rumbula and Bikernicki. Notorious is the so-called "Operation Dünamünde", during which around 3,000 people were murdered in the Bikernicki Woods in the spring of 1942.[121]

---

[121] Andrej Angrick, Peter Klein, *Die "Endlösung" in Riga, ["The Final Solution in Riga"]*, Darmstadt 2006, p. 344: see also Hans-H. Seiffert, "A Jewish Woman from Sehnde ...", pp. 58-62.

There is more information and certainty about the fate of daughter Lisel. Documentation shows that she was taken from Lithuania to the concentration camp Stutthof on July 19, 1944. Upon her arrival there, she was given Prisoner Number 49,103 and was entered in the registry as a laborer. She died there on January 6, 1945[122] – only a few days before Camp Stutthof was evacuated on January 25, 1945.

Undocumented and still unsettled is how Lisel died in Stutthof – whether through disease, debilitation or even violence. Nor has it been possible to find any documents or witness accounts shedding light on how Lisel survived in the ghetto and in the Kaiserwald concentration camp – nor why she finally went from Latvia via Lithuania to Stutthof.

One starting point for a conjecture fitting Lisel's fate is that the SIPO of Kauen (Kaunus) sent her to Camp Stutthof. During an evacuation of the Riga-Kaiserwald Camp, the normal route was with a transport by ship across the Baltic Sea to Danzig. From there, it was a short route to Camp Stutthof. The evacuation of the Jewish prisoners from Riga began only in August 1944. But Lisel arrived in Stutthof in July 1944 already.

It could be that the young woman was already transferred from Riga to Lithuania in May 1944 – to Krottingen, a satellite camp of the Riga-Mühlgraben Camp, not far from the Lativian border. This transfer occurred with the following background: In Krottingen (Lithuanian *Kretinga)* was a branch of the Armeebekleidungsamt (ABA) (Army Clothing Office) in Riga-Mühlgraben. This branch was built there in the spring of 1942. It is possible that Lisel was assigned to this work commando as a trained tailor.

While she was still in the ghetto, she and 1,300 other prisoners[123] had to march under strict security to the ABA satellite camp. In the evening, they all returned to the ghetto. When the Riga Ghetto was closed in the summer of 1943 and the prisoners were transferred to the concentration camp Riga-Kaiserwald, the daily march to the work site stopped. The prisoners then had to spend the nights in two huge sleeping halls, men and women separated, in Mühlgraben.

As of May 1944, 200 men and women were transferred from the ABA Mühlgraben to the ABA Krottigen. There they repaired old uniforms and clothing. Lisel was probably part of this group of 200 internees.

---

[122] Information by the Archives Muzeum Sztutowo, June 20, 2017.

[123] See Franziska Jahn, in: Wolfgang Benz, Barbara Distel, *Der Ort des Terrors, Geschichte der Nationalsozialistischen Konzentrationslager, Band 8 [The Place of Terror, the History of the Nazi Concentration Camps, Volume 8].* München 2005, p. 79.

In June 1944, as the Red Army steadily advanced toward the Baltic States, the Kauen SIPO headquarters ordered the liquidation of the Krottigen satellite camp and the deportation of the prisoners to Stutthof. The fact that Lisel subsequently survived half a year in the "hell of Stutthof"[124], can surely be attributed to her having to do essential work either in the women's section of the tailor shop or in the camp kitchen. That meant she was more or less shielded from the arbitrary murder operations of the kapos[125] and overseers.

In the internment camps of Vichy-France, the situation remained calm far into the next year. It was only in August 1942, that the deportations from the Free Zone of France to the extermination camps of the East were begun. They were launched by a visit of a German-French commission under the leadership of SS Captain Theodor Dannecker on July 15.[126] Shortly before that, the Vichy government under President Pierre Laval had agreed to allow 10,000 foreign and stateless Jews to be deported from the Free Zone to the camps in the East.

In Paris, Dannecker prepared the "final solution" for the Jews in France, and on his tours of the camps in the Free Zone, he wanted to get an overview of the number and condition of those Jews able be deported. In his conversations with camp directors, he learned that HICEM had made available large amounts of money for the emigration of Jews. Thereupon, Dannecker stated his decision in his travel log that *"world Jewry needs to be clear that Jews in the German sphere of control are going to their certain destruction."[127]*

---

[124] Witnesses like Gertrude Schneider, Gerda Wasserman, Jeanette Wolff and others have reported that the living conditions in Stutthof were much worse than in the Riga Ghetto and in Camp Kaiserwald. They and other survivors called Stutthof "Hell"; see Hans-H. Seiffert, *(A Jewish Woman from Sehnde ...)* pp. 73/74. Hermann Kuhn, *Stutthof, ein Konzentrationslager vor den Toren Danzigs [Stutthof, a Concentration Camp before the Gates of Danzig]*, Bremen 1995, p. 134.

[125] A kapo is a functionary prisoner, who could punish and even kill at will.

[126] Dannecker was the leader of the *Judenreferat* [Jewish Department] with the SIPO/SD for France/Belgium.

[127] Obschernitzki, *op. cit.*, p. 267.

```
    MINISTÈRE DE L'INTERIEUR                    Application des Instructions de la Circulaire
    ...........                                 N° 86 Pol.2 du 9/8/1942 ( Paragraphe, rémunéra
    ...........                                 tion des Hébergés) et circulaire N° 294 Pol.
    ...........                                 . du .5/4/1942, de Monsieur le Conseiller
                                                d'État, Secrétaire Général pour la Police.

            BORDEREAUX DES SOMMES VERSEES AUX HEBERGES du CAMP
            POUR LA PERIODE du MOIS DE AOUT 1942.

                         -o-o-o-o-

                  '  CHAPITRE  L.J.I.  '
```

N° Mat.	Noms et Prénoms	Emploi	Total	Emargement
.700	Steinmetz	Hans	Bois	176.-	
..7	Rauch	Leib	"	116.-	
IIo5	Hurwitz	Ludwig	"	100.-	
.60	Segalis	Chaima	"	192.-	
II70	Moler	Joseph	"	40.-	
17..	Gunter	Cohn	"	120.-	
.472	Goldberg	Junkiel	"	192.-	
IIo.	Guggenheim	Dagobert	"	100.-	
.I7o	Desseler	Walter	"	120.-	
I...o	Salomon	Louis	"	120.-	
.c.0	Cymbalista	Jakob	"	120.-	
I.I.	Berberich	Walter	"	100.-	
.bo4	Fest	Wolfgang	"	120.-	
.I..	Alexander	Simon	"	3o6.-	
17o4	Epstein	Ernst	"	120.-	
.7I	Vitcheff	Litlien	"	960.-	
I..7	Reinsberg	Heintz	"	120.-	
Io.8	Fridmann	Oskar	"	120.-	
907	Bier	Rudi	"	120.-	
..78	Hochberger	Simon	"	80.-	
.I14	Cohn	Ludwig	"	96.-	
.o77	Klaymann	Machek	"	312.-	
.oI0	Schudmak	Samuel	"	96.-	

```
                         à reporter....          4.006.-
```

Payroll for forestry work for the month of August 1942 (the last month), listing Dagobert Guggenheim (Photo source: AD Marseille)

If the Guggenheims actually anticipated a solution of such a radical nature has not been preserved for posterity. But they would have sensed an impending disaster when, on August 3, 170 men of the Groupes Mobiles de Réserve (GMR), looking like SS units in their black uniforms, surrounded the camp and forbade anyone from leaving. There was now no chance for escape.

Theodor Dannecker, Leader of the Jewish Department with the SIPO/SD for France
(Photo source: Serge Klarsfeld, *Le Calendrier* [The Calendar of Events])

The chronology of events during the scant two weeks when the Guggenheims were still alive cannot be determined in regard to the individual fates of the three family members. In contrast to Johanna Hammel of Konstanz, whose last letters before and during her trip into destruction were preserved,[128] the author could not fall back on reports of victims or witnesses. There are, however, descriptions of eye witnesses who make the course of the deportation clear for individual victims in Les Milles.[129] From these, it is possible to reconstruct with some accuracy Toni's, Salomon's and Dagobert's journey into death.

The Vichy regime's decision to deport the Jews interned in their sphere of control was now briskly carried out by the ancillary police stations. On August 3, 1942, the police commissioner of Marseille, Maurice de Rodellec du Porzic, outlined the actions to be taken prior to the deportations under the code name *Bringing Families Together* with an announcement stamped *GEHEIM* [SECRET] to the head commissar of Aix-en-Provence. On August 4, 1942, all internees outside of Les Milles were seized in a sweeping operation and brought to the camp. Within the scope of this round-up, Toni Guggenheim was transferred from Hotel "Terminus" in Marseille to Les

---

[128] Seiffert, *Entrechtet-verschleppt-ermordet*, p. 48.
[129] Diary of pastor Henri Manen and description of Rabbi Israel Salzer, in Edwin M. Landau/Samuel Schmitt, *Lager in Frankreich* [Camps in France] (Mannheim: 1991), p. 55ff. and p. 96ff.; excerpts from *Bericht* [Account] Hans Fraenkel, in: Obschernitzki, *op. cit.*, pp. 248, 289; Grandjonc, Grundtner, *op. cit.*, p. 366ff.

Milles.[130] At noon on the same day, trucks and buses brought back all the inmates engaged in farm and forestry work. Among them was Dagobert Guggenheim.

At the same time, the camp administration in Les Milles received an order to make available a list of names for the imminent transfer of the Jews to the occupied zone.

Also on August 4, 1942, the police headquarters in Vichy issued a dispatch to the prefects listing the names of those to be deported, as well as specifying exemptions to the regulation. One important exemption criterion was an age limit. Children under 18 without parents were not to be deported and, according to Number 1 of this directive, *elders over 60 years* were also exempted, which was to the benefit of Salomon at close to 65. The reasons for this exemption not being put into effect with Salomon, as well as several others of this group, will be explained later.

On August 6, 1942, the selection process was begun for the first deportation transport to depart Tuesday, August 11. Additional transport trains were to take all the Jews from Camp Les Milles on August 13 and at the beginning of September. It was now a matter of identifying all those from among the 1,432 internees who were fit for deportation.[131] Tasked with this assignment was Louis Gaudé, head of the emigration department in Les Milles. The Jewish organizations, especially HICEM, were involved in identifying – with a questionnaire created by them – the "special cases" not deemed fit for transport. It must be noted here that all the work would prove useless, since most of these cases were rejected by the Marseille police prefecture without checking.

Collaboration of the Marseille Prefecture with the Nazis

For the first transport on August 11, there were 262 internees selected by alphabetical order of all those with A to G and some H surnames. With the sequential numbers 235 to 237, Salomon, Toni and Dagobert were among them. The list contains various misspellings and inaccuracies probably repeated in typed versions from the original lists. Thus, Salomon's and Dagobert's places of birth, Randegg and Donaueschingen, are not recognizable, whereas Toni's date of birth is incorrect (see photo).

---

[130] The hotel "Terminus des Ports" confirmed the date of departure as August 4, 1941. In the literature the transfer date is also cited as the evening of August 3. See Grandjonc, Grundtner, *op. cit.*, p. 376.

[131] Number of people on August 6, 1942. See Obschernitzki, *op. cit.*, p. 284.

LISTE DES 2&2 ISRAELITES PARTIS EN CONVOI DU

CAMP DES MILLES LE II AUT I942 A DESTINATION DE CHALON-SUR-SAONE.

- ٦ -

AS	Prénoms	P.	Nté	Date Nais.	Lieu Nais.	OBSERVATIONS
	DSCHMIDT	Hans Kurt		All.	8.8.03	Breslau
	GOLDSCHMIDT	Yvan		Aut.	6.7.94	Lubeck
	GOLDSCHMIDT	Erwin	7.	All.	I0.5.23	
2I4	GOLDSTEIN	Lazar		Aut.	23.I.85	Lomberg
2I5	Gossels	Frédéric		All.	29.8.07	Einden
2I6	-LEVY	Anny	Ep.	All.	I3.9.C7	Cologne
2I7	GOTTESMANN	Moses		Aut.	6.2.92	Bouryalaw
2I8	GOTTFRIED	Moses Michel		Aut.	I0.6.88	Vassiléf
2I9	GOTTLIEB	Arnold		Pol.	I5.8.08	Cracovie
220	GREILSAMER	Max		All.	6.3.77	Dreisach
22I	-ROSENBAUM	Clara	Ep.	All.	9.4.90	
222	-GREILSAMER	Richard		All.	22.2.24	
223	GROSS	Hans		Aut.	3I.5.22	Vienne
224	GROSS	Max		All.	I0.4.90	Frankfurt
225	-GROSS	Greta	Ep.	All.	I6.2.95	
226	GROSSBARD	Henri		Aut.	3.I2.84	Varsovie
227	GRUENEBAUM	Simon		All.	I5.5.8I	Weskhein
228	-SAMUEL	Héléne	Ep.	All.	I3.5.8I	Karbach
229	GRUNHAUS	Gada		Rus.	I.I2.02	Varsovie
230	GRUENWALD	Walter		Aut.	8.3.II	Vienne
23I	GUTFELD	Reynold		All.	I2.I0.02	Grobziezno
232	-GUTFELD	Judith		All.		
233	GUTH	Abraham		All.	I6.7.06	Dobrombil
234	GUTTMANN née SEELIEGMAN	Selma		All.	5.7.88	Ichenhausen
235	GUGGENHEIM	Salomon		All.	27.9.77	Kaudegg
236	GUGGENHEIM	Tony	M.	All.	29.7.07	
237	-GUGGENHEIM	Dagobert	Fs	All.	27.7.I0	Bonenscliligen
238	HAAS	Edwin		All.	30.8.04	Bottigheim
239	HAAS	Ernst		All.	I2.6.06	Neustadt
240	HAAS	Salomon		All.	I8.2.79	Rungheim
24I	+ABRAHAM	Mélanie	Ep.	All.	6.2.94	
242	HAAS	Lota		All.	4.I0.2I	

Les Milles deportation list to Drancy from August 11, 1942 with Salomon, Toni and Dagobert Guggenheim (Photo source: AD Marseille)

The total of 185 expatriated Germans represented the largest contingent of deported Jews in Les Milles. Added to them were 55 Austrians and 22 "Eastern Jews." Of the 66 women on this transport, including Toni Guggenheim, 22 of them had been brought from the Marseille hotels to Les Milles only a few days before.

The train left Les Milles at 8 a.m. on August 11. It had been filled the day before. Already by the afternoon of August 10, the people selected for the first transport were led to the station and loaded into eight cattle cars awaiting them. They stayed there with locked doors and without light for the whole night; 28 people, women and men, were in each car. The only "comfort" was the straw spread on the floor. Around 11 p.m., Quaker employees passed out food, water and pails for their bodily needs into the cars for them. Before their departure the next day, they received coffee from the canteen as their last handout.[132]

The inmates on the train no longer had any illusions about the alleged "bringing families together" as the real purpose for the relocation. The announced travel destination, Chalon-sur-Saône, was the border city on France's occupied zone demarcation line. That served as a signal to everyone that they were being taken back into the Nazi rulers' direct sphere of power.

Confronted with this prospect, some of the internees already made suicide attempts during the selection process on the afternoon of August 11 in the open space of the brickyard where two people died.

Among the 262 forced travelers from Les Milles were 35 people, including Salomon Guggenheim, who came under the so-called "elders paragraph" of the August 4 exemption regulation. With strict adherence to the directive, these 35 Jews, aged 60 to 80, would not have been extradited to the German occupation forces. The elders of the next transport suffered the same fate on their transport two days later on August 13. On that one were the selected internees with last names H to Z. Among them was the Konstanzer Hans Picard, an agemate of Dagobert Guggenheim. Since this transport of 538 people was larger, the share of the disregarded exemption cases must also have been larger than the previous transport. The flouting of the exemption regulation, which also applied to children under 18 and sick people, had tragic consequences for all those affected, for they were immediately murdered in the gas chambers of Auschwitz and other extermination camps in the East.

---

[132] Hans Fraenkel eye witness account, in Obschernitzki, *op. cit.*, p. 289

It is documented in research and newspaper reports that in the course of the deportations of Jews from the Free Zone carried out as of July 1942, the exemption regulations for "elders" were definitely applied by the Vichy authorities. The author researched actual instances of the Konstanz Jewish woman Lina Hammel and Leopold Spiegel, both interned in Gurs.[133]

Why did the camp and police forces in Les Milles tasked with drawing up the deportation lists not use the opportunity to apply the exemption paragraph generously to relieve some of the oppressive burden they must have felt when sending the Jews to their deaths? Were they exclusively under the yoke of the German occupation? Or did an anti-Semitic attitude affect the actions of the responsible Vichy officials on site in such a way that they only used the chance of saving the over-60-year-olds – and the other noted exemption cases in the August 4 dispatch – in a negligent way?

The reports of the clergymen Henri Manen and Israel Salzer, as well as the journalist Hans Fraenkel, all of whom were witnesses to the deportations, agree that the directive about the exemption cases was made known to the camp administration in Les Milles only as of August 13 and 14, 1942, that is, *after* the departure of the second deportation train.[134] Therefore, Camp Director Robert Maulavé, who in contrast to his superiors in Marseille treated people humanely, had no back-up in the form of an official directive to intervene on behalf of "special cases."

Louis Gaudé, the head of the emigration office in Les Milles, made known after the end of the war during a hearing in the trial of high Vichy officials that, in August 1942 with the decision of the deportation of the Jews, there was no thought given to making any exemptions.[135] If exemptional provisions were nevertheless issued but were not immediately made available to the authorities responsible for implementing the deportation, the seemingly strict regulations break down on the side of arbitrariness.

Two men were responsible for delaying the exemption directive transmission: Marseille Prefecture Police Stations Director Rodellec du Porzic and Head of Security Robert Auzanneau. Both were known to be anti-Semitic and for advocating for a speedy "solution to the Jewish problem." Both men understood their role in the bureaucratic process of the deportations to be not mere transmitters of instructions from their superiors in the Vichy administration offices. Rather, they played an active and leading role in the deportation of the Jews from Les Milles. Already in July

---

[133] Seiffert, Entrechtet-verschleppt-ermordet ....., pp. 33 and 37.
[134] Grandjonc, Grundtner, *op. cit.*, p. 425.
[135] Obschernitzki, *op. cit.*, p. 280.

1942 they had – in quasi-anticipatory duty – voluntarily submitted proposals to the Vichy Interior Ministry containing specific details about the number of the deportees, as well as schedules and transport conditions. With its complicit Jewish policies, the leadership of the Marseille prefecture made itself an active collaborator of the Holocaust that the Germans set in motion. Theodor Dannecker, the Nazi representative responsible for this "project" in France, was able to achieve the high success rates he reported to Berlin because the Vichy-enacted exemption directive was initially ignored by the Marseille police department. Paradoxically, the higher Vichy authorities gave the police department carte blanche by granting them judicial powers to let them freely decide the exemption cases.[136] This power was extensively used by Robert Auzanneau – tragically to the disadvantage of many deportees who could have stayed behind, Salomon Guggenheim among them.

Unknown, however, is whether Salomon Guggenheim actually would have remained behind had he qualified as a "special case." After all, he would have had to live with being separated from his wife Toni and nephew Dagobert. There are reports from the same Gurs deportation as to which exempted husbands freely chose to go with their families to the camps in the East. One of these selfless and devoted men was the Konstanz lawyer Leopold Spiegel, a campmate of Salomon during their Gurs internment.[137]

Final Destination of Auschwitz-Birkenau on August 14, 1942

After the train with the Guggenheims departed from the Les Milles station at 8 a.m. on August 11, only a few intermediate stops were made on the way to the Auschwitz final destination. Probably none of the unfortunate passengers had any idea that they had only five more days to live.

The train's first stop was Sorgue-Châteauneuf-du-Pape at 11:10 a.m. where a train from Rivesaltes with 520 passengers from other countries was hitched on. From there, the route continued to Chalon-sur-Saône to Drancy in the Occupied Zone, the collection camp near Paris. The precise arrival at

---

[136] Grandjonc, Grundtner, op. cit., p. 374.
[137] Leopold Spiegel shared the same fate as his college friend, the Mannheim pediatrician Julius Strauss. See Seiffert, op. cit., p. 37; Ludwig Mann, Martyrium und Heldentum in Gurs [Martyrdom and Heroism in Gurs], in E. R. Wiehn, Camp de Gurs 1940. (Konstanz: 2000), pp, 152-153.

the Le Bourget-Drancy station is recorded as 8:13 a.m. on August 13, f[138] or the 650-kilometer trip the train had taken an entire day. It must have been an extremely exhausting journey under terrible conditions.

The entrance area of Camp Drancy upon arrival (Photo source: Serge Klarsfeld, *Le calendrier* [The Calendar of Events])

The stay at Camp Drancy was of short duration for most of this train's passengers. Of the 782 people arriving by several transports from Les Milles, 749 were already forced into a "connecting train" to the Auschwitz-Birkenau destination two days later. The interruption of the trip to Auschwitz was necessary for collecting and forming new groups of deportees. There were technical reasons too, however: In Drancy the Jews were

---

[138] Serge Klarsfeld, *Les transfers de juifs de la région de Marseille vers les camps de Drancy ou de Compiègne en vue de leur déportation 11 août 1942 - 24 juillet 1944* [The Transfer of the Jews from the Marseille Region to Camp Drancy or Compiègne on the Way to their Deportation August 11, 1942 – July 24, 1944] Paris: 1992).

transferred to German freight trains made available by the *Wehrmacht* [Army] traffic authority. German military personnel now took over guarding the transports to the extermination camps. With that, the Jews having been expelled and expatriated from Germany were again at the mercy of the Nazi henchmen.

On the morning of August 14, 1942, Transport 19 left Drancy station. The precise departure of train 901/14 was recorded as 8:55 a.m. A total of 1,015 Jews were crammed into the cars. The escort personnel for the transport into death was not provided by the SS, but by soldiers of the Wehrmacht, who, in this way, also made their contribution to the implementation of "the Final Solution". Sergeant Kropp was responsible for the train supervision.

The special feature about this transport was its being the first record of carrying children under the age of 12, opening a cruel new dimension in the deportation process from France to the East,[139] though none of the children of this transport came from Camp Les Milles.

Noteworthy about the telex message of the SS office in Paris to Berlin is also the instruction to send along "as usual" food rations for two weeks on the transport to Auschwitz. This was done with the certain knowledge that most of the deportees would have only a life expectancy of two days. That is how long the transport took. Upon arrival at Auschwitz, those not fit to work were immediately sent to the gas chambers. Obviously, the "generous" food allocations served only to mask the true intentions of the "final solution" perpetrators.

The transport list was comprised of five sublists in which surnames, first names, date of birth, place of birth and nationality were documented. Among them are the names and data of Salomon, Toni and Dagobert Guggenheim. The list of the Guggenheims repeats the same mistakes as on the one issued in Les Milles. Clearly, the information was transferred unchecked from list to list.

The Guggenheims were accompanied on their way to Auschwitz by other Konstanzers: Laura Ferber (61), Manja Goldlust (48), Jeannette Kletschoff (57) and Rosa Moerschner (56).

---

[139] The head of the Jewish Department in France, SS Captain Heinz Röthke (successor to T. Dannecker) on August 14 reported via telex to Adolf Eichmann in Berlin and the Auschwitz Camp Commandant the deportation of 1,000 Jews, "children among them for the first time." See Schaubild, source: *ITS Internationaler Suchdienst* [International Search Service], Bad Arolsen.

R.F. ⚡⚡

Sicherheits=Dienst
Nachrichten-Uebermittlung

Aufgenommen				Befördert				Raum für Eingangsstempel
Tag	Monat	Jahr	Zeit	Tag	Monat	Jahr	Zeit	
				14. Aug. 1942				
von		durch		an		durch		

Verzögerungsvermerk

Nr. 16008

Telegramm — Funkspruch — Fernschreiben — Ferospruch

IV. J   SA 225 a   Paris, den 14.8.1942
He/Bir

                          Dringend, sofort vorlegen !   . heim!

An das
Reichssicherheitshauptamt, Referat IV B 4,
z.Hd. ⚡-Obersturmbannführer EICHMANN, o.V.i.A.
B e r l i n

An den
Inspekteur der Konzentrationslager
in Oranienburg

An das
Konzentrationslager
in A u s c h w i t z

        Am 14.8.1942, 8,55 Uhr hat Transportzug Nr. D. 901/14
den Abgangsbahnhof Le Bourget-Drancy in Richtung Auschwitz mit
insgesamt 1000 Juden verlassen. (Darunter erstmalig Kinder)
Der erfaßte Personenkreis entspricht den gegebenen Richt-
linien.
        Transportführer ist Stabsfeldwebel K r o p p , dem
namentliche Transportliste in zweifacher Ausfertigung mitge-
geben wurde.
        Mitgegebene Verpflegung wie üblich pro Jude für
Tage.

                                            I.A.

                                    Röthke.
                          ⚡ - Obersturmführer

Operations confirmation by the Paris Gestapo office to the RSHA Berlin of the Transport 19 departure to Auschwitz (Photo source: ITS Arolsen). There were four other Konstanz women (p. 97) Manja Goldlust (48), photo see p.143.

After a two-day trip, the train arrived at Camp Auschwitz-Birkenau on August 16, 1942. No oral or written witness reports are available about the fate of the Guggenheims, as for instance what happened upon arrival at the infamous ramp of the Auschwitz-Birkenau train station. The commendable analyses of the SS bureaucracy's records by Serge Klarsfeld and Danuta Czech,[140] as well as requests by the author to the information centers at Auschwitz and the Red Cross did not yield any reliable information. But Serge Klarsfeld's analyses from the available accompanying documents, as well as the reports about the arrival of Transport 19 in Auschwitz, allow for drawing conclusions with a high degree of probability.

Selection at the ramp at Auschwitz-Birkenau (Photo source: Serge Klarsfeld, *Vichy – Auschwitz*)

Not confirmed is whether all 1,015 deportees who left Drancy arrived alive at Auschwitz. It happened frequently that people weakened from the rigors of the trip died on the way. It is also important to note that 115 men between the ages of 18 to 42 were selected for labor at the Auschwitz-Birkenau ramp. The men were given the registration numbers 59229 to 59343. All the others

---

[140] S. Klarsfeld, *Les transferts des juifs de la région de Marseille vers les camps de Drancy ou de Compiègne en vue de leur déportation 11 août 1942-24 juillet 1944, Paris 1992*; Danuta Czech, *Kalendarium der Ereignisse im Konzentrationslager Auschwitz-Birkenau 1939-1945* [Calendar of Events in the Concentration Camp Auschwitz-Birkenau 1939-1945]. Frankfurt/M., 1989.

were killed in the gas chambers on the same day. It is a certainty that Salomon and Toni Guggenheim were among that group of victims.

Dagobert Guggenheim had just turned 32 and therefore fit into the age group of the 115 selected men. One document, in which the selected men were listed by name is no longer traceable, according to information from the Muzeum Oswiecim [Auschwitz Museum]. But a meticulous count of the birth dates on the deportees' list confirms that the number of 115 selected men is only correct if Dagobert is part of it. Thus, it can be assumed that Dagobert was assigned to the work detail at the Birkenau ramp on August 16, 1942.

Selection for work detail in Auschwitz (Photo source: Serge Klarsfeld, *Additif au Mémorial*)

Nr. 32951/1942 (1393)   C¹

Auschwitz, den   2.Oktober _____ 19 42

D   er rbeiter Hans Picard _____

_____ mosaisch _____

wohnhaft Konstanz, Franz Seltestraat 16 _____

ist am   26.September 1942 _____ um ___ 09 ___ Uhr ___ 25 ___ Minuten

in   Auschwitz, Kasernenstrasse _____ verstorben.

D   er Verstorbene war geboren am   22.März 1910 _____

in   Konstanz _____

(Standesamt _____ Nr. _____)

Vater : Ludwig Picard _____

Mutter : Melanie Picard geborene Guggenheim, wohnhaft ____

in Marseille _____

D   Verstorbene war nicht verheiratet

_____

Eingetragen auf mündliche schriftliche Anzeige   des rztes Doktor der ___

Medizin Kremer in Auschwitz vom 26. eptember 1942 _____

D   Anzeigende _____

_____

Vorgelesen, genehmigt und   unterschrieben

D e Übereinstimmung mit dem
Erstb uch wird beglaubigt.

Auschwitz, den   2.10. 19 42

Der Standesbeamte   Der Standesbeamte
In Vertretung   In Vertretung
                               Quakernack

Todesursache: Herzwassersucht _____

Eheschliessung de   Verstorbenen am_____ in _____

(Standesamt _____ Nr. ____)

Death certificate of Hans Picard at Auschwitz (Photo source: Muzeum Oswiecim)

This is where all attempts at interpretations and speculations about his fate end. There is no trace giving details about the place and exact time of his death. In this regard, the search for clues differs from that of his Konstanz agemate Hans Picard. Picard, who was mentioned earlier, was brought with the second deportation train from Les Milles to Drancy and was assigned to Transport 20, departing Drancy on August 17, 1942, and arriving at Auschwitz on August 19. The 32-year old Konstanz man was also selected for the work detail and lived in Auschwitz for just over a month. He died on September 26, 1942.[141]

Further research showed that of the 115 selected men from Transport 19, only the Polish Jew Nathan Seroka survived Auschwitz-Birkenau. It is certain that Dagobert Guggenheim died at Auschwitz. Whether he died of debilitation or was killed by the camp staff remains as much a question as the time of his death.

In the course of the reparation court case brought by the Argentine relatives, the Konstanz Court on November 26, 1953 declared Dagobert dead. The official date of death was set at December 31, 1945[142] – a completely unrealistic date, given the research results from today's standpoint.

The Survivors in Argentina and the USA – Desperate and Irreconcilable

It was reported that Isi Guggenheim,[143] upon receiving the news about the deportation and murder of his parents at Auschwitz, was overcome by a deep and long-lasting despair. Despite his continually going to the immigration agencies and pushing hard for his parents' entry permits, he now had to acknowledge that his efforts with the bureaucracy in far-away Argentina were not sufficient. Emigration by legal means – still relatively easy in his case in 1938 – succeeded in only a few cases by mid-1941 when the "final solution of the Jewish question" through mass executions of the SS-task force units in Eastern Europe was already underway. And those emigrants who did get out were usually prominent or very wealthy people who were able to do so with the help of influential sponsors at the point of departure and in the host country.

---

[141] Baden-Württemberg State Archives, *Die Opfer* ... [The Victims ...], *op. cit.*, p. 272, see also death certificate Auschwitz camp.
[142] Freiburg State Archives, File F 196/1, No. 5800.
[143] Statements by daughter Gabriela Guggenheim, letter of April 8, 2008.

The great majority of emigrants who were still able to reach safe havens by mid-1941 owed this feat largely to the aid organizations for Jews operating in the Marseille area. Examples are HICEM, UGIF (General Union of Jews in France), HIAS, the famous JOINT[144] and the Emergency Rescue Committee (ERC) with Varian Frey, their leader in France. Relying on unofficial and covert operations, they were successful – usually by illegal means – in bringing quite a few Jews at risk of deportation to safety, even in 1942.[145]

Only those internees in Les Milles who could find escape agents with the financial help and connections of influential friends abroad were able at this point to elude the Vichy regime's police forces, the complicit agents of the Nazi henchmen. Clearly, neither Isi Guggenheim nor the family of his aunt Bona Guggenheim in Buenos Aires could muster such powerful leverage.

It is not known whether the Guggenheims also looked for every last straw in the wind, which other rescuers living in Argentina had grasped to help their relatives with emigration from Europe. One saving straw could be obtained by the submission at the Argentine Ministry of Agriculture, whereby the immigration application would be based on the immigrant having specialized knowledge and the willingness to contribute to the urgently needed development of the country's agriculture. It was well-known that the liberal Minister of Agriculture, who was also in charge of the Immigration Office, handled such applications with more generosity. In just this way, Kurt Löwenstein, one of Isi Guggenheim's boyhood friends from Konstanz, was able to bring his parents to Argentina in 1940.[146]

Rather, Isi and Bona's family were hoping until the end that the authorities in France and Argentina would allow make possible the departure of their relatives to Argentina in compliance with the prescribed procedures. Had they known about the official emigration prohibition for Jews enacted by the collaborative Vichy regime at the end of June 1941,[147] the Guggenheims in Argentina would have realized that this hope was deceptive.

The news of the deportation of the two men – Salomon and Dagobert – to Auschwitz, as well as Toni with her cardiac condition, triggered the worst

---

[144] American Jewish Joint Distribution Committee was an aid organization of U.S. Jews with worldwide activities.

[145] In this way, the following prominent Jews could attribute their eventual flight to the ERC: Heinrich and Golo Mann, Hannah Arendt, Lion Feuchtwanger, Marc Chagall, Max Ernst and Franz Werfel with his wife Alma Mahler.

[146] Written report by Liliana Löwenstein, daughter of Kurt Löwenstein at the laying of Stolpersteine (commemorative brass plaques) in Konstanz, October 5, 2015.

[147] See chapter "Long Months ... in Les Milles"

fears among the relatives in Argentina. Rumors had even reached this far abroad that many Jews had died in that camp. Nevertheless, the Argentines probably still kept their hopes up.

Subsequently, it is probably Isi who first realized that his elderly parents had no chance of survival. In the case of the younger and stronger Dagobert, the relatives could hope that, until the end of the war, he had survived in a work crew at Auschwitz and would still be found alive by the liberators upon the liquidation of the concentration camp in January 1945. But this glimmer, too, died at the end of the war when there was no sign of Dagobert being alive throughout 1945.

The Guggenheims in the safety of Argentina then knew that the Auschwitz labor and extermination camp had become the end station of their family members Salomon, Toni and Dagobert.

Isi Guggenheim, though safe from the persecutors' physical access, continued to be the victim of the Nazi policies at an emotional level. The fact that he had not been able to save his parents from being deported and murdered in Auschwitz plagued him for a long time. He considered this to be a personal failing, continually blaming himself, even within his family. Like other Jews, too, who were the only ones to escape the Holocaust, Isi continued to live with the guilt feelings that he had not been at the side of his parents until the bitter end.

The ongoing despair resulted in his being unable to reconcile himself with his hometown of Konstanz and the new, democratic Germany for the rest of his life.

He ignored the documents that the Konstanz District Council Office repeatedly requested during 1960 for the purpose of re-naturalization.

Isi saw his hometown only once more when he visited there upon an invitation by the city in 1973. But the reunion ended in disappointment, as Isi did not feel welcomed. He felt estranged and lonely, not the least because he had the impression that the few people who still knew him from before tried to avoid him.

His Aunt Bona also was not able to return to Donaueschingen after the war, neither as a visitor nor a resident to the place that had been her home for so long.

Fritz Rosenwald, too, who, in the US had fought until the bitter end with his time and money for an entry visa for his sister Lisel, was weighed down after the failure by feelings of despair in that he was unable to get at least one family member – in this case, Lisel – to the "safe harbor" of New York.

With the imminent entry of the USA into the world war, his mental and physical powers were directed to a new assignment – Fritz, alias Fred Rosenwald, was drafted into the US Army and had to fight against his old homeland at various places in Europe. He was even stationed in Germany toward the end of the war and thus helped liberate Germany from the regime that had persecuted and driving his own family to death.

Fritz Rosenwald as a soldier in the US Army in Augsburg, July 1945 (Photo source: Joan Fradkin)

While the war still raged, Fritz married Ruth Finger, a German Jewish woman from Essen, who had been managed to flee to the USA in 1938. The couple had two children after the war – son Charles and daughter Joan.

After the connection with his family had been suspended as of the end of November 1941, Fritz had no further news about their fate until long after the end of the war. He had to assume, therefore, that they became victims of the Holocaust. The final information came from a lawyer[148] hired to do research, who reported in February 1962 that the parents and Lisel were deported to Riga and did not return.[149]

The So-called "Reparations" in Post-War Germany

On July 31, 1957, through his attorneys in Buenos Aires and Frankfurt/Main, Isi Guggenheim applied for compensation for his parents' "deprivation of liberty," as well as his father's "loss of professional advancement" through the District Court of Restitution in Freiburg/Baden.

In November and December 1958 – after more than a year – Isi received the first notifications from the court authority for both parents that he was awarded 3,300 DM each for loss of liberty. The calculation was based on a period of imprisonment from October 1940 to the end of August 1942.

Isi's attorneys contested this decision, however, by pointing out that it was not certain that both parents had not survived Auschwitz until the end of the war. Rather, May 8, 1945 should be the assumed date of death. The Restitution Court rejected the plaintiffs' claims on the grounds that the documents accompanying the transport to Auschwitz did not allow for this conclusion. Only 115 men were selected and, according to empirical evidence, an age limit of up to 45 years had been applied. For Toni and Salomon Guggenheim, therefore, the date of death of August 1942 had to be assumed. As unacceptable as the small compensation amounts were, establishing the date of death as August 1942 must be deemed correct by today's research findings.

Much later, in April 1963, Isi received a decision about his father's "loss of professional advancement," that Salomon Guggenheim was prevented from working in his profession from January 1939 until his death in August 1942, and a compensation of 4,782 DM was set.[150]

The Donaueschingen Guggenheim family also claimed compensation for the injustices they suffered. In April 1950, Bona, who had fled to Argentina, submitted a legal challenge for the 1938 forced sale of the property in Donaueschingen. The Konstanz District Restitution Chamber declared the sale contract of August 31, 1938 and the subsequent property registrations to be null and void. With the signing of a new purchase contract in 1950, the

---

[148] Letter of attorney Carl Loeb, Cologne, February 9, 1962, in: Rosenwald Family Papers, Affidavits and Correspondence for Visa, item 18.
[149] About the fate of the Rosenwalds, see chapter " Shattered Hope for Emigration. ..."
[150] Freiburg State Archives, Reparations File F 196/1, Order No. 9611 and 10031.

property, which had been badly damaged at the end of the war, was revalued. As a result, the former owners received an additional payment for the much too low selling price of 1938.

Destroyed Guggenheim department store in Donaueschingen, 1945 (Photo source: Donaueschingen City Archives)

This restitution claim was recognized comparatively quickly. Already in 1947, the French military government enacted an ordinance (No. 120) whereby "stolen property" was to be returned. Thereupon, the "Baden State Office for Controlled Assets" in Donaueschingen had immediately taken control of the property.

The transfer back to the former Jewish owners came within the time frame whereby Bona could still benefit from the restitution.

The former company property in the Singen Scheffelstrasse, however, was not refunded to the former Jewish business partners. An out-of-court settlement could be reached with the later owner, however, whereby compensation was also paid in this case for the reduced price realized on the forced sale. In addition, Bona applied to the State Office for Restitution in Freiburg for compensation for herself and Dagobert, who had been murdered in Auschwitz, for various financial and income losses suffered by mother and son as a result of flight and deprivation of liberty.

The processing time of these applications through the German State Office for Restitution in Freiburg turned out to be extremely lengthy. Bona had to ask her attorney in Germany several times to speed up the case. Still, it took eight years before the first decisions about the Bona and Dagobert's restitution case were made. On September 25, 1958, the restitution amount of 9,224 DM for loss of capital, emigration costs and the destruction of their household was set.

Bona herself no longer benefited from this remuneration: She had died six years before in December 1952 in Buenos Aires. She had named her daughter Erna Strauss as the sole heir.

From 1959 to 1968, additional restitution payments pertaining to the Nazi regime's special taxes (Jewish asset tax, tax for household goods, forced payments to the Jewish Council and the Jewish religious community) were granted, as well as the already mentioned damages from deprivation of liberty and loss of professional advancement. The payments amounted to a total of 15, 584 DM.[151] By the time the last payment arrived, Erna Strauss, too, had died in July 1968. She had transferred her claim to her son, Alfred Strauss, also living in Argentina. From start to finish, the examination and assessment processes had taken so long that two generations of the applicants' party could no longer benefit from the compensation.

The Guggenheims undoubtedly shared the fate of many of those persecuted by the Nazis. Most of the restitution applicants had the impression that the judges and officials were trying to dismiss or reduce their claims or delay their cases. One of the Allied military government's expert commissions, for example, determined that "a completely outmoded and unmotivated judiciary sees no need for a timely settlement of numerous claims for refunds."[152] One of the reasons was the continuation of the same personnel in the judiciary as well as in the regional tax offices. If someone formerly responsible for the expropriation of Jewish property was now processing the reparation claims in the Restitution Office, it is clear that this person had now developed a vehement defensiveness.

Whether this continuation of personnel was the cause of the delayed completion in the case of the Guggenheims' restitution could not be proved.

---

[151] Freiburg State Archives, Reparations File F 196/1, Order No. 5800

[152] Jürgen Lillteicher, *Die Rückerstattung in Westdeutschland, zitiert bei Sebastian Stiekel: Arisierung und Wiedergutmachung in Celle* [Restitution in West Germany, cited by Sebastian Stiekel: Aryanization and Reparations in Celle], (Bielefeld: *Verlag für Regionalgeschichte* [Publisher for Regional History], 2008), p. 114.

The unusually long procedure – also in comparison to Isi Guggenheim's modest request – led to the suspicion that the responsible officials treated an "unpleasant" dossier as a secondary matter.

Was a full "restitution" made upon the completion of the reparations case? Certainly not. Both the compensation-in-kind granted (such as in the rather rare cases of restitution of former assets) as well as the compensation paid in the majority of cases[153] are purely material acts of justice, that is, an attempt to approximately restore the former asset status of those persecuted by the Nazis. They are no more than a symbolic gesture by which the Baden Administrative District acknowledges the guilt of its Nazi predecessor administration.

Genuine reparation involves human initiatives, approaching those who were expelled from their neighborhoods and personally offering to take them back into their former circle of friends and acquaintances. For non-Jewish citizens, a prerequisite is, of course, that they show a much-needed empathy, an understanding of the psychic wounds of those who were ostracized from their midst years ago, and the willingness to take the returnees gently by the hand and lead them back into their community.

In the case of Isi Guggenheim's return in 1973, his former acquaintances in Konstanz, as well as his schoolmates and neighbors, unfortunately had not yet reached that level of supportive assistance. This may be due to the shame and sense of guilt based on the simple fact of not having resisted or criticized the persecution of their Jewish fellow citizens.

The Guggenheims' reconciliation with the city of Konstanz resulting from a successful "partial restitution" took place only with the next generation, when Isi's daughter Gabriela Guggenheim visited Konstanz in May 2009 upon the invitation of the Konstanz *Stolpersteine* Initiative. This gave her a chance to visit the building in which her father was born in the Hüetlinstraße and to participate in the laying of memorial stones for her grandparents Salomon and Toni, for her father Isi, as well as memorial stones for the Donaueschingen relatives Bona and Dagobert.

---

[153] For capital compensation, the conversion ratio was 10 RM (Reichsmark) to 2 DM (Deutschmark).

Isi Guggenheim with daughter Gabriela (right) and granddaughter Maia, 1998 (Photo courtesy of Gabriela Guggenheim)

From the protection of time and space, and with the composure of a generation not directly affected by the persecutions of the Nazi rulers, Gabriela was able to give a hopeful outlook for future cooperation with the people of Konstanz:

It was an important experience for me to visit the city of my ancestors for the first time...and...to learn various aspects of my family that my father had not shared because it was too painful for him to dig into the past. ...I hope to visit your beautiful city again with my daughters, so that they may know the city of their grandfather [Isi–Ed.].[154]

---

[154] Written statement by Gabriela Guggenheim, June 16, 2009 to the Konstanz *Stolpersteine* Initiative.

Gabriela Guggenheim at the laying of the memorial stones for her relatives in the Konstanz Hüetlinstraße 21, May 2009 (Photo credit: H.-H. Seiffert)

Biographical Data about the Guggenheims and Rosenwalds

Salomon Guggenheim
- Born: September 27, 1877 in Randegg
- Last freely chosen residence: Konstanz, Hüetlinstraße 21
- Soldier: World War I
- Residence at time of deportation: Konstanz, Zogelmannstraße 16
- Deportation to Camp Gurs: October 22, 1940
- Transfer to Les Milles transit camp: March 1941
- Deportation to Auschwitz extermination camp: August 14, 1942
- Declared dead; assumed date of death: August 16, 1942

Toni Guggenheim, née Jung
- Born: June 29, 1891 in Gailingen (sister of Bona Guggenheim)
- Married: Salomon Guggenheim, 1913
- Residence in Konstanz and deportation to Gurs → see Salomon Guggenheim
- Internment in Hotel "Terminus des Ports," Marseille (satellite camp of Les Milles): March 1941 to August 5, 1942
- Deportation to Auschwitz and murder → see Salomon Guggenheim
- Declared dead; assumed date of death: August 16, 1942

Isi Guggenheim
- Born: April 20, 1915 in Konstanz (son of Salomon and Toni Guggenheim)
- Emigrated to Buenos Aires, Argentina: June 1938
- Established a career as an entrepreneur in the packaging industry
- Marriage to Annemarie (née Ziegel) of Berlin; two daughters: Silvia and Gabriela
- Died: May 7, 2000 in Buenos Aires

Abraham Guggenheim
- Born: February 6, 1874 in Gailingen
- Established a clothing department store in Donaueschingen, Wasserstraße, with Hermann Einstein of Konstanz: 1897
- Established two branch stores in Singen and Gaggenau: 1899 and 1900
- Purchased property in Donaueschingen's Max-Egon-Straße and transfer from Wasserstraße: 1906
- Soldier in World War I as a storm trooper on the Eastern front

- Died: December 1, 1932 in Donaueschingen
- Buried in the Gailingen cemetery

Bona Guggenheim, née Jung
- Born: December 21, 1881 in Gailingen (sister of Toni Guggenheim)
- Married: Abraham Guggenheim of Gailingen
- Residence in Donaueschingen: Max-Egon-Straße 14 until November 1938
- Partner in the clothing department store in Donaueschingen, Singen and Gaggenau
- Residence in Konstanz (in her sister's household): November 1938 to December 1939
- Emigrated to Buenos Aires, Argentina: December 1939
- Died: December 11, 1952 in Buenos Aires

Erna Strauss, née Guggenheim
- Born: September 18, 1905 in Donaueschingen, daughter of Abraham and Bona Guggenheim
- Married: Ludwig Strauss
- Son: Alfred Strauss, born March 6, 1933
- Emigrated to Argentina: 1935
- Died: July 19, 1968 in Buenos Aires

Dagobert Guggenheim
- Born: July 27, 1910 in Donaueschingen (son of Abraham and Bona Guggenheim)
- In "protective custody" in the Dachau concentration camp: November 11, 1938 to December 20, 1938
- Moved to Konstanz, Hüetlinstraße 21: December 22, 1938
- Residence in Zogelmannstraße 16: November 17, 1939
- Deportation to Gurs, transfer to Les Milles and deportation to Auschwitz → see Salomon G.
- Date of death: unknown
- Officially declared dead: December 31, 1945

Fritz (Fred) Rosenwald
- Born: May 11, 1915 in Cologne
- Emigrated to the USA in March 1938, residence in New York City
- Drafted into the US Army during World War II with deployment in Europe 1944/45

- Married Ruth Finger (a German Jewish woman from Essen) in September 1943, two children: Charles (born 1948) and Joan (born 1951)
- Died February 1, 1992 in New York City

Lisel Rosenwald
- Born: June 3, 1914 in Cologne
- Residence in Cologne, Antwerperner Straße 32, last at Bismarckstraße 10
- Profession: milliner
- Deportation to Riga (Ghetto) on December 7, 1941
- Died: January 6, 1945 in Camp Stutthof

Karl Rosenwald (Father of Fritz and Lisel)
- Born: November 18, 1879 in Cologne
- Residence: see Lisel R.
- Cognac DistilleryOwner
- Deportation to Riga (Ghetto) on December 7, 1941
- Did not survive; date of death and place – unknown

Johanna Rosenwald (Mother of Fritz and Lisel)
- Née Ledermann on August 26, 1890 in Meiningen
- Residence: see Lisel R.
- Deportation to Riga (Ghetto) on December 7, 1941
- Did not survive; date of death and place – unknown

Chronology of the Lives of the Guggenheims and Rosenwalds during the Nazi Regime

1933

- **March 6:** Alfred Strauss, son of Erna Strauss (née Guggenheim) is born in Frankfurt/Main.
- **April 1:** The Guggenheims' department stores are affected by the Nazi regime's call for a boycott. The Guggenheim Company business partners – the widows Bona Guggenheim and Klara Einstein, and Mr. Emil Frank – thereupon make the following decisions:
- **September 21:** The Guggenheim Company moves its headquarters from Donaueschingen to Singen.
- **November 2:** Partner Emil Frank gains a third of the business property in Donaueschingen

1935

- **February:** Fritz Rosenwald accepts a position in Konstanz with the "Schweizer Lohnstickerei" Company and becomes friends with Isi Guggenheim.
- **September:** Erna Strauss emigrates to Buenos Aires, Argentina with husband Ludwig and son Alfred.
  - Lisel Rosenwald visits her brother Fritz in Konstanz and meets the Guggenheims of Konstanz, as well as Isi's cousin Dagobert.

1938

- **February 28:** The Gaggenau branch of the Guggenheim department store is "Aryanized."
- **March 18:** Fritz Rosenwald lands in New York City after departing Hamburg on the steamship *Manhattan*
- **April 19:** Isi Guggenheim leaves his position with the Hermann Einstein Company in Konstanz and in May emigrates to Argentina on the ocean liner *Jamaique*.
- **June 2:** Isi Guggenheim arrives in Buenos Aires.
- **September 21:** The Singen branch of the Guggenheim department store is sold to the Muck & Co. business.
- **October 1:** The property in Donaueschingen is sold to the mineral water manufacturer Anton Volk.

- **October 8:** The business in Donaueschingen is transferred to businessman Willi Schuler.
- **November 9/10:** *Reichspogromnacht* [Regime's *Kristallnacht*]: Bona Guggenheim's residence in Donaueschingen is destroyed.
- **November 11:** Dagobert Guggenheim is taken into "protective custody" and brought to the Dachau concentration camp.
- **November 21:** Bona Guggenheim moves in with her sister Toni and brother-in-law Salomon on Hüetlinstraße in Konstanz.
- **December 20:** Dagobert is released from Dachau and also moves in with the Konstanz relatives on Hüetlinstraße.

1939
- **As of February:** Bona, Toni, Salomon and Dagobert Guggenheim submit emigration applications to Argentina and Chile.
- **November 17:** All four Guggenheims are forced to move to Zogelmannstraße 16, Konstanz.
- **December 4:** Bona Guggenheim emigrates to be with her daughter Erna in Argentina.

1940
- **March 1:** The Rosenwald family is forced to move to Lindenburger Straße in Cologne.
- **September 8 – 24:** Lisel sees Dago for a last time on her visit to Konstanz.
- **October 22 –** *Bürckel-Wagner-Aktion*: Toni, Salomon and Dagobert Guggenheim are deported with about 6,500 other Jews of Baden and Saarpfalz to Camp Gurs in southwest France.

1941
- **February 28:** Toni and Salomon Guggenheim transferred to Les Milles transit camp near Aix-en-Provence
- **March 2:** Toni is interned in Hotel "Terminus des Ports" in Marseille, a satellite site of Camp Les Milles.
- **March 16:** Dagobert Guggenheim arrives in Camp Les Milles.
- **June 18:** The Rosenwalds are forced to move to Bismarckstraße 10.
- **July 1:** Salomon writes to the Jewish Community in Kreuzlingen to thank them for a financial donation.
- **December 7:** Deportation of Karl, Johanna and Lisel Rosenwald to Riga.

1942

- **January 20:** Wannsee Conference in Berlin: Agreement is reached for the organization of the *Final Solution of the Jewish Question*.
- **July:** Foreign Jews, even from France's "Free Zone," are deported to the extermination camps in the East.
- **August 4:** Toni Guggenheim is transferred from Marseille to Les Milles and meets Salomon and Dagobert there.
- **August 11:** Deportation of the three Guggenheims by train to the Drancy collection camp near Paris.
- **August 14:** Toni, Salomon and Dagobert are deported from Drancy to Auschwitz-Birkenau on Transport No. 19.
- **August 16:** Auschwitz arrival: Salomon and Toni Guggenheim immediately gassed there. Dagobert is presumably "selected" for labor, though his fate is unknown.

1943

- **February 18:** Fred Rosenwald is drafted into the US Army.

1944

- Fred Rosenwald is deployed to Europe as a US soldier.
- **July 19:** Lisel Rosenwald is taken to the concentration and extermination camp Stutthof.

1945

- **January 6:** Lisel Rosenwald dies in Camp Stutthof

Source and Literature Index

Unpublished Sources

Aide Aux Émigrés Section Suisse from February 5,

Archives Départementales (AD) Des Bouches-du-Rhône, Marseille, "Borderaux des Sommes Versées aux Hébergés du Camp des Milles," File 142 W 29.

Camp Gurs Directorate. Request on February 1941 to the prefects of the Départments Basses Pyrénées for transfer of Salomon and Toni Guggenheim to Les Milles, AD Basses Pyrénées, Pau, France.

- Request of March 8, 1941 for transfer of Dagobert Guggenheim to Les Milles, AD Basses, Pyrénées, Pau.

Donaueschingen City Archive. March 2, 2009 written information.

Einstein, Firma Hermann. Report of April 4, 1938 for Isi Guggenheim. Konstanz. Gabriela Guggenheim private archive.

Fradkin, Joan, Letter of February 3, 2019 to the author

Freiburg State Archive. Restitution File F196/1, No. 5800.

- Restitution File F196/1, No. 9611.

- Restitution File F196/1, No. 10031.

Gaggenau City Archive. July 2, 2009 letter.

Guggenheim, Dagobert, Letter of November 30, 1941 to Fritz Rosenwald

Guggenheim, Gabriela, Letter of April 8, 2008 to the author

- Letter of June 16, 2009 to the Konstanzer Stolperstein-Initiative

Guggenheim, Salomon, Letter of July 1, 1941 from Les Milles

ITS International Search Service, Bad Arolsen, Cover letter for the transport list No.19 of Drancy to Auschwitz

- Registration book for Dachau concentration camp

Konstanz City Archive. File "Law pertaining to Leases with Jews."

Löwenstein, Liliana, report about the laying of Stolpersteine in Konstanz, October 5, 2015.

Muzeum Oswiecim. Death certificate of Hans Picard (January 8, 2010 email)

Muzeum Sztutowo, information to the author, June 20, 2017.

Published Sources

Badische Zeitung [Baden Newspaper], November 10, 1992.

DIE ZEIT [German weekly newspaper], No. 28/1998

Donaueschinger Tagblatt [Donaueschingen Daily Paper], November 25, 1932.

Katalog der Ausstellung zur Wannsee-Konferenz und dem Völkermord an den europäischen Juden, Berlin 2008 (Exhibition Catalogue of the Wannsee Conference and the Genocide of European Jews, Berlin 2008).

Reichsgesetzblatt [Reich's Law Gazette 1938] I, Ordinance about the Registration of Jewish
Property.

Rosenwald Family Papers – Collections Search-United States, https://collections.ushmm.org/search/catalog/im73437.

Schwarzwälder Tagblatt [Black Forest Daily Paper], March 31, 1933; April 8, 1933; October 7, 1938.

Literature

Angrick, Andrej, Klein, Peter, *Die "Endlösung" in Riga [The "Final Solution" in Riga]*, Darmstadt 2006.

Baden-Württemberg State Archive Directorate (ed.). *Die Opfer der nationalsozialistischen Judenverfolgung in Baden-Württemberg 1933-1945* [The Victims of the Nazi Persecution of Jews in Baden-Württemberg 1933-1945]. Stuttgart: 1969.

Benz, Wolfgang, Distel, Barbara, *Der Ort des Terror, Geschichte nationalsozialistischen Konzentrationslager, Band 8 (The Place of Terror, the History of the Nazi Concentration Camps, Volume 8), München 2005.*

Birnbaum, Suzanne. *Une Francaise juive est revenue* [A French Jewish Woman Came Back]. Paris: Hérault Éditions, 1989.

Bloch, Erich. *Geschichte der Juden von Konstanz* [The History of Jews in Konstanz]. Konstanz: 1971.

Buch der Erinnerung. Die ins Baltikum deportierten deutschen, österreichischen und tschechoslovakischen Juden, Bd. 2 [Memorial Book. The German, Austrian and Czechoslovakian Jews deported to the Baltic Region, Vol. 2], K.G. Saur, München 2003,

Corbach, Dieter, *6.00 Uhr ab Messe Köln-Deutz, Deportationen 1938-1945 [6:00 a.m. from the Messe Cologne-Deutz, Deportations 1938-1945], Cologne 1999.*

Czech, Danuta. *Kalendarium der Ereignisse im Konzentrationslager Auschwitz-Birkenau 1939-1945* [Calendar of Events in Auschwitz-Birkenau Concentration Camp 1939-1945]. Frankfurt/Main: 1989.

Friedrich, Eckhardt, and Dagmar Schmieder. *Die Gailinger Juden* [The Jews of Gailingen]. Konstanz: *Arbeitskreis für Regionalgeschichte e.V.* [Work Group for Regional History, 1981.

Gedenkbuch [Memorial Book], Information from the State Archive of Cologne, Notebook 77, Cologne 1995.

Grandjonc, Jacques, and Theresia Grundtner. *Zone der Ungewissheit, Exil und Internierung in Südfrankreich 1933-1945* [Zone of Uncertainty, Exile and Internment in Southern France 1933-1945]. Rowohlt, Reinbek, 1993.

Groszman, Gabriel, Semi Uffenheimer, *Jüdische Familiengeschichten aus Breisach, Lörrach, Bühl, Graben in Baden und in Argentinien [Jewish Family Stories of Breisach, Lörach, Bühl, Graben in Baden and in Argentina]*, Konstanz 2013.

Guéno, Jean P., and Jérôme Pecnard. *Paroles d'étoiles, l'album des enfants cachés (1939-1945)* [Words from the Stars, the Hidden Children's Album (1939-1945)]. Paris: Éditions des Arènes, 2002.

Gutterman, Bella, and Naomi Morgenstern. *The Gurs Haggadah*. Jerusalem, Yad Vashem: Devora Publishing, 2003.

Huth, Volkhard. *Donaueschingen, Stadt am Ursprung der Donau* [Donaueschingen, City at the Source of the Danube], Sigmaringen: Jan Thorbecke Verlag, 1989.

-   *Erinnerungen und Gegenwart, Historische Wegweiser durch Donaueschingen* [Memories and the Present, Historic Guide Through Donaueschingen]. City of Donaueschingen: 1992.

Kappes, Reinhild. *... Und in Singen gab es keine Juden?* [...And in Singen There Were No Jews?]. Sigmaringen: Jan Thorbecke Verlag, 1991.

Klarsfeld, Serge, *Additif au mémorial de la déportation des juifs de France* [Addition to the Memorial of the Deportation of the Jews of France]. Paris: 1978.

-   *Le calendrier de las persécution des juifs de France, Juillet 1940 – août 1942* [Calendar of Events of the Persecution of the Jews of France, July 1940 – August 1942]. Paris: 2001.

-   *Les transfers de juifs de la région de Marseille vers les camps de Drancy ou de Compiègne en vue de leur déportation 11 août 1942 – 24 juillet 1944* [The Transfer of Jews of the Marseille Region to the camps Drancy or Compiègne for Deportation on August 11, 1942 – July 24, 1944] Paris: 1992.

- *Vichy-Auschwitz*. Hamburg: Dephi Politik, 1989.

Kuhn, Hermann, *Stutthof, Ein Konzentrationslager vor den Toren Danzigs,* [*Stutthof, a Concentration Camp before the Gates of Danzig*], Ed. Temmen, Bremen 1995.

Laharie, Claude. *Gurs: 1939-1945*. Biarritz: Atlantica, 2005.

Landau, Edwin M., and Samuel Schmitt. *Lager in Frankreich* [Camps in France]. Archive Directorate Stuttgart, *Dokumente über die Verfolgung der jüdischen Bürger in Baden-Württemberg durch das Nationalsozialistische Regime 1933-1945, Band 2* [Documents about the Persecution of Jewish Citizens in Baden-Württemberg by the Nazi Regime 1933-1945, Volume 2]. Stuttgart: 1966.

Obschernitzki, Doris. *Letzte Hoffnung – Ausreise, Die Ziegelei von Les Milles, Aix-en-Provence 1939-1942* (Last Hope – Emigration, The Brickyard of Les Milles, Aix-en-Provence 1939-1942). Teetz: Hentrich & Hentrich, 1999.

Rügert, Walter, ed. *Jüdisches Leben in Konstanz* [Jewish Life in Konstanz]. Konstanz: UVK-Verlag, 1999.

Sauer, Paul. *Die Schicksale der jüdischen Bürger Baden-Württembergs während der nationalsozialistischen Verfolgungszeit 1933-1945* [The Fates of the Jewish Citizens of Baden-Württemberg during the Time of Nazi Persecution 1933-1945]. Stuttgart: 1969.

Schott Dieter, and Werner Trapp. *Konstanz in den 20er und 30er Jahren* [Konstanz in the 1920s and 1930s]. Konstanz 1985.

Seiffert, Hans-Hermann. *Entrechtet – verschleppt – ermordet, Der Weg einer Konstanzer Jüdin Johanna Hammel in die Gaskammer von Auschwitz-Birkenau* [Disenfranchised – Deported – Murdered: The Journey of the Konstanz Jewish Woman Johanna Hammel to the Gas Chamber of Auschwitz-Birkenau]. Konstanz: 2007.

Seiffert, Hans-Hermann, *A Jewish Woman from Sehnde Comes Back, Gerda Rose Survives the Nazi Death Camps Jungfernhof, Kaiserwald and Stutthof as well as the Death March, Hartung-Gorre Publishing, Konstanz/Germany 2018.*

Stiekel, Sebastian. *Arisierung und Wiedergutmachung in Celle* [Aryanization and Restitution in Celle]. Bielefeld: *Verlag für Regionalgeschichte* [Publisher for Regional History], 2008.

Von zur Mühlen, Patrik. *Fluchtziel Lateinamerika, Die deutsche Emigration 1933-1945* [Safe Haven Latin America, The German Emigration 1933-1945]. Bonn: 1988.

Vormeier, Barbara. *Die Deportationen deutscher und österreichischer Juden aus Frankreich* [The Deportation of German and Austrian Jews from France]. Paris: 1980.

Wiehn, Erhard Roy. *Oktoberdeportation 1940* [October 1940 Deportation]. Konstanz: 1990.

Camp de Gurs 1940. Konstanz: 2000.

- *Die bittere Not begreifen. Deutsch-jüdische Deportiertenpost aus südfranzösischen Internierungslagern, [Understanding the Desperate Need. German-Jewish Deportation Mail from Southern French Internment Camps]*, Konstanz: 2016.

Zahlten, Richard, *Dr. Heinrich Feurstein.* Donaueschingen 1992.

Additional Photos and Documents

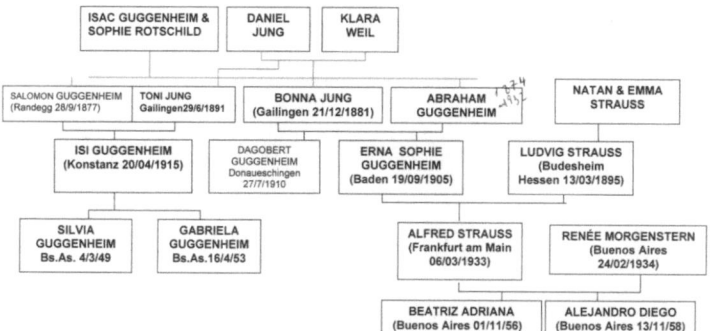

Guggenheim-Strauss Family Tree
(Courtesy of Gabriela Guggenheim Archive)

Salomon and Isi Guggenheim, circa 1937 (Photo courtesy of Gabriela Guggenheim Archive)

Dagobert Guggenheim with nephew Alfred Strauss, circa 1935 (Photo courtesy of Beatriz Strauss Archive)

Isi Guggenehim with his wife Annemarie, circa 1946 (Photo courtesy of Gabriela Guggenheim Archive)

Isi and Annemarie Guggenheim with daughter Silvia, circa 1952 (Photo courtesy of
Gabriela Guggenheim Archive)

Silvia and Gabriela Guggenheim, vacation at the beach, circa 1956 (Photo courtesy of
Gabriela Guggenheim Archive)

Guggenheim & Cie. Store Opening, Donaueschingen (Photo source: *Donaueschinger Wochenblatt*, February 13, 1932)

Guggenheim Department Store in Donaueschingen Announcement (Photo source: *Donaueschinger Tagblatt*, November 25, 1932)

Donaueschingen und Baar

Donaueschingen, 2. Dez. (Todesfall.) Heute Nacht
starb, ohne vorher ernstlich krank gewesen zu sein, an
einem Schlaganfall Herr Kaufmann Abraham Guggenheim im Alter von 58 Jahren. Der Verstorbene war als Kaufmann in Stadt und Bezirk und da-
rüber hinaus eine bekannte und geachtete Persönlichkeit.
Im Jahre 1897 nahm er in Donaueschingen seinen
Wohnsitz und gründete hier in dem Hause, das heute
Kaufmann Theodor Maier bewohnt, ein Kurzwaren-
geschäft. Da dieses rasch emporblühte, waren neue
Räume notwendig, Herr Guggenheim entschloß sich
1900 zur Errichtung des heutigen großen Geschäfts-
gebäudes, in dem er seinen Betrieb auf weitere Bran-
chen ausdehnen und somit seinen Kundenkreis bedeutend
erweitern konnte. Auch in den schweren Zeiten des
Weltkrieges tat der Verstorbene als Soldat seine Pflicht,
er stand bei einer Landsturmformation an der Front
im Osten. Der so jäh in Trauer versetzten Familie
wendet sich allgemeine Teilnahme zu. Das Andenken
des Verstorbenen, der als pflichtbewußter Bürger galt,
wird in Ehren gehalten werden. — Die Bekanntgabe
über Zeit und Ort der Beisetzung erfolgt in der mor-
gigen Nummer.

Obituary of Abraham Guggenheim Photo source: *Donaueschinger Tagblatt*, December 12, 1932)

Translation:

Donaueschingen and Baar

Donaueschingen, Dec. 2 (Bereavement) The businessman Abraham Guggenheim died during this night of a heart attack at the age of 58 without having been seriously ill. As a businessman, the deceased was a well-known and respected personality in the city, the district and beyond. He moved to Donaueschingen in 1897 and established in this house – now occupied by businessman Theodor Meier – a haberdashery and notions store. As this store grew rapidly and new space became necessary, Herr Guggenheim decided in 1900 to erect the current large commercial building in which he could expand his business and enlarge his customer base. Even during the hard times of the World War, the deceased did his duty as a soldier and was active in a militia unit on the Eastern front. The family, which is so suddenly plunged into mourning, accepts the public's condolences. The memory of the deceased, a devoted citizen, will be remembered with honor. An announcement about the time and place of the funeral will appear in tomorrow's edition.

Guggenheim Department Store in Gaggenau (upper left) (Photo source: Festschrift Badischer Sängerbund 1925 [Commemorative Publication of the Baden Sängerbund 1925])

Guggenheim Department Store in Singen, circa 1900 (Photo source: Kappes, ... *Und in Singen* ... [...And in Singen...])

Zeppelin-Oberrealschule mit Realgymnasium Konstanz

Abgangs-Zeugnis.

Guggenheim Isi   isr. Bek.

geboren den *20. April 1915* in *Konstanz*

~~Sohn~~ des *Kaufmanns Salomon Guggenheim,*
~~Tochter~~

besuchte unsere Anstalt vom *29. April* 19*25* bis zum *24. März* 19*31*

in den Klassen *Sexta* bis einschl. *Unter-Sekunda* in der Oberrealschul-Abteilung,

in den Klassen ——— bis einschl. ——— in der realgymnasialen Abteilung.

Am Unterricht der zuletzt genannten Klasse nahm $\frac{er}{sie}$ seit *Ostern 1930* teil.

$\frac{Er}{Sie}$ erhielt nach Konferenzbeschluß vom *23. März 1931* folgende Noten:

Betragen . . :	*Gut*	Physik . . . . . . :	*Gut*
Fleiß . . . . . . :	*Gut*	Mathematik . . . :	*Gut*
Leistungen . . :		Zeichnen . . . . . :	*Hinlänglich*
		Schreiben . . . . . :	
Religion . . . . . :	*Sehr gut*	Turnen . . . . . . :	*Hinlänglich*
Deutsch . . . . . :	*Sehr gut*	Singen . . . . . . :	*Ziemlich gut*
Französisch . . . :	*Gut*		
Englisch . . . . . :	*Gut*	*Freiwillige Fächer:*	
Latein . . . . . . :		Latein . . . . . . :	
Geschichte . . . . :	*Gut*	Griechisch . . . . :	
Erdkunde . . . . :		Italienisch . . . . :	
Naturgeschichte . . :		Kurzschrift . . . . :	
Chemie (Mineralogie, Geologie)	*ziemlich gut*		

Versetzung betr.: *Wird versetzt*

Bemerkung . . : *Besitzt die mittlere Reife*

Konstanz, den *27. März 1931.*

Die Direktion: Der Klassenvorstand der $U\,\overline{II}$:

Dr. E. Fuchs,
Lehramtsassessor.

Report Card for Isi Guggenheim from the Zeppelin-Oberrealschule [High School], March 27, 1931 (Photo courtesy of Gabriela Guggenheim Archive)

Report Card for Isi Guggenheim from the Konstanz Trade School, March 19, 1932 (Photo courtesy of Gabriela Guggenheim Archive)

131

15. III.

II4/Rfl

Steuerliche Unbedenklichkeitsbescheinigung.
Gegen die Auswanderung des Salomon G u g g e n h e i m,
geb. am 27.9.1877 zu Randegg, zuletzt wohnhaft Konstanz,
Hüetlinstr.21, sowie gegen die Mitnahme von Umzugsgut nach
dem Ausland bestehen keine steuerlichen Bedenken.

In Vertretung:

Landesarchiv Baden-Württemberg
Staatsarchiv Freiburg

Alle Rechte vorbehalten

Bestand: F 196/1 Nr. 96 11

Tax document stating that there are no outstanding debts for Salomon Guggenheim,
March 15, 1939 (Photo source: Freiburg State Archive)

Gravestone of Adele Rothschild (sister of Salomon Guggenheim), Gurs Cemetery, 2009
(Photo credit: H.-H. Seiffert)

Transcription of Salomon Guggenheim's Letter from Les Milles on July 1, 1941

Salomon Guggenheim
Group A3
Camp Des Milles

At the Rh. (Bouches du Rhône)   July 1, 1941

Dear Frau Veit!

I, and also in the name of dear Tony, thank you and the Women's Organization there most sincerely for the generous donation of money that you sent and which has now come into my possession.

We don't have enough words of gratitude for you and the esteemed Women's Organization for your kind donations that you have now sent in a most loving manner for a third time.

Our wish to be with our dear Isi soon, has, unfortunately, not been fulfilled, since we need our passports to register for the visas and the Konstanz Passport Office is not giving them back, despite complaints lodged by various parties. Our Isi has done everything possible and has prepared everything for us. These difficulties placed upon us are a great concern to us and are a big detriment to dear Tony's health, as she already had problems with her heart.

May God somehow find a way for us to fulfill our much longed-for wish.

Again, dear Frau Veit and the much appreciated Women's Organization, [we send– Ed.] our heartfelt thanks with sincere greetings from your grateful Tony and Salomon Guggenheim.

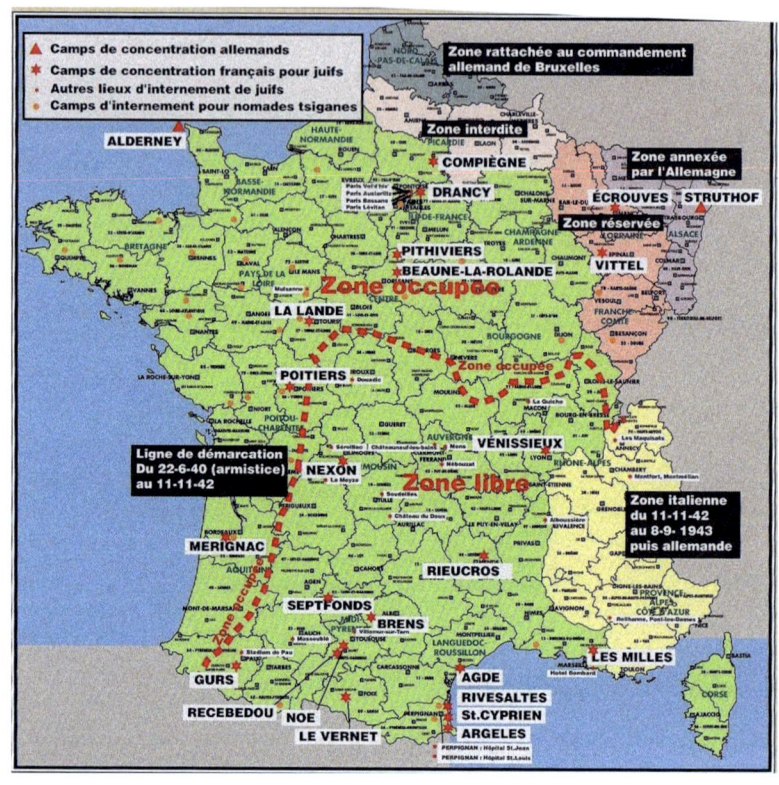

Internment Camps in France 1939-1944 (Photo source: Guéno/Pecnard, *Paroles d'étoiles*)

Internment identification pass of Dagobert Guggenheim in Les Milles with camp number 1153 (Photo source: AD, Marseille)

A work commando of Jewish women in Riga at the corner of Valnu Iela (Wall Street) and Teatra Iela (Theater Street) in 1943/44 (Photo-Source: Haus der Wannsee-Konferenz, Berlin)

KZ-Stutthof, Prisoner Identification Cards of Lisel Rosenwald from 1944/07/19 (Photosource: Muzeum Sztutowo)

Repatriation offer to Isi Guggenheim of September 15, 1960 (Photo courtesy of Gabriela Guggenheim Archive)

Translation:
Application for reacquisition of
German citizenship
through naturalization

We request a reply to our air mail letter of July 18, 1960 – II d/E. If our office does not hear from you by October 15, 1960, we assume that you are not interested in a reacquisition of German citizenship and [therefore] consider our naturalization application as withdrawn.
Signed I.A. Schmidt
Government Head Inspector

Postcard of Buenos Aires in the 1940s (Photo source: H.-H. Seiffert Archive)

From left: Erika Rosenberg, Hans-Hermann Seiffert, Gabriela Guggenheim, Henri Pechtner in Buenos Aires, March 2008 (Photo source: H.H.Seiffert)

Gabriela Guggenheim and Beatriz Strauss in Buenos Aires, March 2008 (Photo credit: H.-H. Seiffert)

From left: Hans-Hermann Seiffert, Valeria Glejzer (Gabriela's daughter), Gabriela Guggenheim, Henri Pechtner in Buenos Aires, March 2008 (Photo source: H.H.Seiffert)

Joan Fradkin Rosenwald, New York 2016 (Photo credit: H.-H. Seiffert)

Hüetlinstraße Konstanz at the end of the 1930s

Toward Bodanplatz and in 2010, and (Photo credit: H.-H. Seiffert, 2010)

Reconstructed Guggenheim department store in Donaueschingen, March 2010 (Photo source: Willi Hönle)

Translation:

Head of Security Police
and SD

Berlin SW 11   October 1940
Prinz-Albrecht Straße 8

IV D4   2602   /40

To the *Auswärtige Amt* [State Department]
Attn: SA Standard Leader Envoy L u t h e r
Berlin

The *Führer* ordered the deportation of the Jews of Baden via Alsace and the Jews of Pfalz (Palatinate) via Lothringen. Upon implementation of the operation, I can report to you that
6,504 Jews
from Baden were deported on October 22 and 23, 1940, with 7 transport trains and from Pfalz on October 22, 1940, with 2 transport trains in agreement with the local offices of the Wehrmacht without prior knowledge of the French agencies to the unoccupied part of France via Chalon -sur-Saône.

The deportation of the Jews was carried out in all parts of Baden without a hitch or any incidents.

The process of the operation was scarcely noticed by the residents.

The collection of Jewish assets, as well as their fiduciary administration and reclamation, will be carried out by the district presidents in charge.

Jews living in mixed-marriages were exempted from the transports.

Letter by Reinhard Heydrich, October 29, 1940

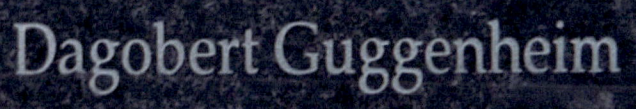

Gurs memorial obelisk in Konstanz at the corner of Bahnhofstraße and Sigismundstraße. On the left is the building of the old Jewish Community of Konstanz (Photos credit: H.-H. Seiffert, March 2010)

1937 Photo of Manja Goldlust (age 48), Konstanz, deported with the Guggenheims on
Transport No. 19 to Paris-Drancy to Auschwitz and murdered there on August 18, 1942
(Photo source: private property)[155]

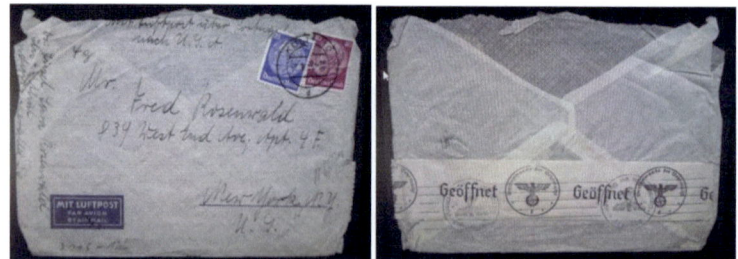

Envelope of letter by Dagobert Guggenheim to Fritz Rosenwald from Camp Les Milles –
with a note about current mail censoring

---

[155] See Manja Goldlust's letters from Gurs to the Kreuzlingen Jewish Community in: Erhard Roy Wiehn
(ed.), *Oktoberdeportationen 1940* (Konstanz: 1990), pp. 721ff., 740, 752ff., 756ff., 758ff.

Camp Stutthof – Prisoner postcard (no name, only a number as identification!); photo source: Stutthof Museum Archive

About the Author

Hans-Hermann Seiffert was born in 1940 in Sehnde, near Hannover, Germany. He received a Master of Business Administration in Göttingen and subsequently held management positions with manufacturing systems engineering companies in southwest Germany. Upon retiring in 2005, Seiffert decided to devote himself to the study, research and publication of the story of National Socialism and the Holocaust.

As a member of the "Stolpersteine for Konstanz – Against Intolerance and Forgetting Initiative," the author published several books, some translated into English, about the fate of the Jews in his current home of Konstanz and his hometown Sehnde.

Other Books by Hans-Hermann Seiffert*:

My Beloved Children! Letters of Hella Schwarzhaupt to Her Children from Gurs and Récébédou Internment Camps, 2015. 128 pages, many photos and documents.
€ 15,30
ISBN 978-3-86628-521-7

Meine geliebten Kinder! Die Briefe der Konstanzer Jüdin Hella Schwarzhaupt aus der Internierung in Gurs und Récébédou an ihre Kinder.
2013. 138 Seiten, zahlr. Fotos und Dokumente.
€ 19,80
ISBN 978-3-86628-486-9

Johanna Hammel. Der Weg einer Jüdin aus Konstanz durch Gurs nach Auschwitz-Birkenau.
Herausgegeben von Erhard Roy Wiehn, 2011. 104 Seiten, zahlreiche Fotos und Dokumente.
€ 14,80 ISBN 978-3-86628-358-9

Johanna Hammel. The Journey of a Jewish Woman from Konstanz via Gurs to Auschwitz-Birkenau, 1898-1942
Published by Improbable Memoirs, Alexandria, VA https://improbablememoirs.com/
2017. 108 pages, many photos and documents.
$16
ISBN 978-0-9966822-1-3

In Argentinien gerettet – in Auschwitz ermordet. Die Schicksale der jüdischen Familie Salomon Guggenheim aus Konstanz und Abraham Guggenheim aus Donaueschingen 1933-1942.
Herausgegeben von Erhard Roy Wiehn. Konstanz 2010. 114 Seiten, zahlr. Fotos und Dokumente.
€ 14,80.
ISBN 978-3-86628-312-1

Entrechtet – verschleppt – ermordet. Der Weg der Konstanzer Jüdin Johanna Hammel
in die Gaskammer von Auschwitz-Birkenau. 1898-1942
Herausgegeben von Erhard Roy Wiehn. Konstanz 2007. 56 Seiten.
€ 9,80
ISBN 3-86628-179-X **(sold out)**

Eine Sehnder Jüdin kommt zurück..
Gerda Rose überlebt die NS-Todeslager Jungfernhof, Kaiserwald und Stutthof sowie den
Todesmarsch
Konstanz, 2016, 129 Seiten.
$19.80
ISBN 978-3-86628-568-2

A Jewish Woman from Sehnde Comes Back.
Gerda Rose Survives the Jungfernhof, Kaiserwald and Stutthof Nazi Death Camps, as
well as the Death March
Konstanz, 2018. 170 pp.
$25.83
ISBN 978-3-86628-611-5

*A listing of Hans-Hermann Seiffert's books is available at: www.hartung-gorre.de/Seiffert_english.htm. His German publisher, Hartung-Gorre Verlag, may be
found online at: www.hartung-gorre.de; email verlag@hartung-gorre.de.